In Search of Hippocrates

A Solution to
The Health Care Crisis Facing
AMERICA

In Search of Hippocrates

A Solution to
The Health Care Crisis Facing
AMERICA
by
Martin J. Collen, MD, MBA
Mark J. Handwerker, BS, PhD

Published by
Martin J. Collen and Mark J. Handwerker

Contact us at ... *insearchofhippocrates@gmail.com*

ISBN: 978-1475253184

ON BEING A DOCTOR

Doctor (Latin, docere) simply means "to teach." Throughout their careers, physicians will learn with and teach their fellow physicians, medical students, and patients. The alleviation of suffering by physicians requires a vast skills-set involving the most advanced technical, scientific, and clinical knowledge, as well as the attributes of empathy and compassion for their fellow humans, as set forth by Hippocrates, "the father of western medicine," in 400 BCE.

The practice of medicine is dependent on the accumulation of an enormous fund of medical knowledge. Advancements in the medical field are achieved primarily through academic and clinical research, as well as anecdotal case histories and reports. In order to acquire and maintain the highest level of current knowledge and expertise, physicians must read and absorb vast quantities of current medical literature, both through attendance at conferences, searching the internet, and consulting with their fellow physicians. This lifelong commitment to learning is essential to becoming the finest physician.

Furthermore, the inquiring physician will vigorously investigate the various mysteries of nature, which have engaged scientists in all ages, in the hope of finding the causes of disease, and developing the means to prevent and cure diseases into the future. Physicians all over the world share these lofty goals.

When taking care of a patient, empathy, understanding, and sympathy are expected of the physician, for the patient is clearly more than the sum of his various symptoms, dysfunctions, and emotions. The ill patient is frightened and vulnerable, and in great need of hope and reassurance from their physician. The strength or weakness of the relationship that is formed between physician and patient will significantly help determine the ultimate outcome of the diagnosis and treatment of the patient's presenting illness. In other words, the physician's support of and caring for their patient, when the patient is most vulnerable, is critical to the patient's sense of well-being throughout their diagnosis, treatment, and recovery.

At each step of the process of caring for their patient, the questions most often asked by astute physicians are "Of what benefit are my various interventions to the patient?" and "Will any of these tests or treatments be potentially more harmful than the condition being treated?" With adherence to the Hippocratic Oath, the physician's most essential obligation is to "do no harm."

DEDICATION

This book is dedicated to the American People
whose creativity and compassion, courage
and perseverance has been -- and always shall be --
of notable merit to the world.

ACKNOWLEDGEMENTS

"I am grateful to the following individuals for their invaluable insights, support, and patience in the preparation of this book: my wife, Roberta J. Collen, BA, MPA, MBA, and our wonderful children, Jacob F. Collen, MD, MAJ, MC, USA; Benjamin R. Collen, 2nd Lt., US Army Reserve, 3rd year Medical Student, David Geffen School of Medicine, University of California, Los Angeles, Anna Collen, Undergraduate, University of California, Riverside."

-- Martin --

"I would like to express my love and appreciation to my wife, Judith, and my children, Margo and Aaron, without whose support and constructive criticism this book could never have been written."

-- Mark --

TABLE OF CONTENTS

Prologue
What is Wrong With Health Care in America?   1

Introduction
What Can We Do About it?   5

Chapter 1
"America, we have a problem."   14

Chapter 2
*The Hippocratic Oath and The Essence
That Defines a Physician*   27

Chapter 3
*Good Science and Technology Are The
Foundations of Good Medicine But Not Its Soul*   43

Chapter 4
*Being A Patient Requires More
Than Just Being Patient*   53

Chapter 5
*A Brief History of Health Care and
How We Got Into This Mess*   78

Chapter 6
The Cost-Drivers of Health Care   108

Chapter 7
*Nothing Less Than a Revolution: A Fair and
Equitable Solution to the Health Care Crisis*   157

Chapter 8
What Would The Founding Fathers Do?   205

Information Resources   221

About the Authors   222

LIST OF TABLES AND GRAPHS

Figure 1 - *Percent of Total Deaths for the 15 Leading Causes of Death for the United States*   58

Figure 2 - *Body Mass Index (BMI)*   66

Figure 3 - *Types of U.S. Physician Practices*   123

Figure 4 - *Annual Cost of Major Diseases*   137

Figure 5 - *Population of U.S. Citizens, 65 Years of Age and Older, by Size and Percent of the Total Population Between 1900 and 2010*   141

Figure 6 - *Top Seven Earning Health Insurance Company Total Premiums Received, Medical Benefits Paid, Medical Operating Costs, and Percent Operating Costs*   151

Figure 7 - *Top Seven Earning Health Insurance Company Total Earned Revenues and Profits from Invested Premiums*   152

Figure 8 - *Personal Health Care Expenditures by Source of Funds in The United States from 1998 to 2008*   155

Figure 9 - *Annual Cost of Major Preventable Diseases*   182

Figure 10 - *2010 Federal Budget Expenditures of The United States of America*   187

Prologue

What is Wrong With Health Care in America?

Medical care in America has never been better. Americans are living longer and healthier, happier and more productive lives. They are more industrious and have more time to realize their dreams. However, with that said, it is clear that the once great service and pleasant courtesy that existed between doctors and patients has never been worse. At the same time, the cost for Health Care in America is spiraling out of control.

How do we as Americans -- with our great heritage and penchant for "doing the right and honorable thing" -- implement and deliver excellent Health Care to all inhabitants of our Nation and still hold Health Care costs at bay?

The perfect "pie in the sky" plan would be to place the problem in the hands of doctors and patients. A solution that would embolden, empower, and motivate Health Care suppliers (doctors) and recipients (patients) to solve medical problems while at the same time reduce Health Care costs. That plan is easier said than done. As the daily principles of civility, punctuality, and professional thoroughness put forth by doctors and insurance carriers, and the cooperation and compliance required of patients, often fall short: a condition that promotes conflict in Health Care delivery at a professional, business, and financial level.

Doctors world-wide in American Medical Schools and medical schools abroad are trained for 7-15 years in the same principles of ethics, compassion, and caring for patients. They are taught astuteness for disease and treatment as put forth by Hippocrates, the father of western medicine, in 400 BCE. This instruction goes hand-in-hand with the goal of producing physicians who can successfully practice state-of-the-art medicine and who -- because of their training, expertise, skill, and efficiency -- should be able to provide excellent medical care for all at the least possible cost. Likewise, patients are constantly being educated in the art and science of personal health maintenance with the daily bombardment of information from television, radio, internet, and newspaper sources: a voluminous Health Care "literature," that teaches us how to take better care of our self and challenges us to be more proactive when it comes to our personal health. The adoption of a take-charge attitude -- that doctors must expect of their patients -- should result in regular physician visits, compliance with directions regarding prescribed medication, and the pursuit of preventative Health Care. However, these simple practices have not evolved to the point of becoming routine because of the continuous interjection into the Health Care mix by insurance and prescription medication carriers whose bogus and redundant requests for authorizations, miscommunications, and denials of care "gum up the works." The atrocious smoke and mirror tactics of medical insurance carriers have caused more than enough chaos in our contemporary Health Care system to make it impossible for the doctor-patient relationship to develop in America in a direction that could result in the continued delivery of better care for all at reduced costs.

Now, let us ask the big question that concerns us all.

Why is it that Health Care in America, when the ability to take care of patients has never been better, is hobbled by lousy service, poor delivery, and out-of-control costs: costs that have never been higher? Why is it -- while the technology, pharmacology, and medical training of our physicians is outstanding -- that the Health Care system in America "stinks."

The present Health Care system in America promotes doctor-patient polarity, which fosters divergence from the primary goals of patient care; miscommunication with regard to doctor's instructions and patient's appointments resulting in medical errors, and litigious concerns and fears. The reason is, in large part, due to the conflict that exists in a Health Care system controlled by insurance companies, public and private business administrators, lawyers and other non-medical participants with no "skin in the game" other than financial gain. A state-of-affairs that ends up awarding minimal control of -- and authority for -- patient care to doctors and patients. In a country that prides itself on being a "free enterprise," "supply and demand system," Health Care in America has become a severely restricted system that excludes many doctors and patients from developing a more healthful doctor-patient relationship. The primary reason for all of this is that Health Care in America is delivered in a vertically integrated Health Care system, which fosters carelessness, overwork, neglect, and greed. Costs increase because of poor motivation by supplier and consumer, and because of fixed, inelastic prices set by those "non-medical participants." Essentially, a "vertically integrated Health Care system" is a "monopoly" that charges what it wants, sees who it wants, and does what it wants with no regard for the simple concepts of cost, excellent service, ethical responsibility, and the caring and compassionate doctor-patient relationship that would, otherwise, be present in a supply and demand system.

The 14th Century, English Franciscan friar and philosopher, William of Ockham, proposed a simple strategy for solving problems that scientists still apply today. It is the principle known as Occam's razor. Occam's razor states the following: *"All things being equal when evaluating two or more competing theories attempting to explain the same phenomenon, it is best to accept the simpler one."* Although Occam's razor was originally used to advance our understanding of nature's physical laws, it works just as well to help us deal with many everyday problems: no matter their level of complexity.

Therefore, the simplest solution would be to create a Health Care system in America that utilizes a horizontally integrated Health Care approach based on free enterprise: a system that would fit more comfortably into the economic fabric of the United States of America.

Introduction
What Can We Do About It?

Since the inception of America in 1776, the American People -- empowered by the ideal and desire to enjoy *"life, liberty, and the pursuit of happiness"* -- have brought about advancements in the field of medicine the likes of which the world has never seen. During the past two hundred years, these advancements have included the improvement and proliferation of the skills of physicians to accurately diagnose and successfully treat their patients. This pursuit of medical knowledge and technology has accelerated exponentially in the past sixty years. In lockstep with those advancements have come the rising costs of Health Care.

Today, those costs amount to nearly $3,000,000,000,000 ($3 trillion): more than one-fifth of our gross national product. These prohibitive and insurmountable expenses have made it necessary for *"We The People"* to rekindle our desire to act boldly in our efforts to keep and secure the American dream by reducing those costs. At the same time, we must do it without sacrificing our liberty. In order to accomplish this task, we must stop all the distracting and useless bickering and focus on the real causes of the incessant rise in Health Care expenditures.

Prior to the 1950's, the major focus in medicine was acute injury and illness. At that time, the modes and practices of surgical techniques, the limited availability of technology and medications such as penicillin, and an inability to provide long-term care, made it practically impossible for physicians to concentrate their attention on chronic disease and, its corollary, chronic disease prevention (preventative medicine). However with the coming of the 1960's, there was an explosion in medical research and technology. Early treatments for such diseases as hypertension, hyperlipidemia, obesity, and diabetes mellitus -- collectively known as *metabolic syndrome* -- made it possible to curtail the development of vascular diseases of the heart and brain, kidney and other major organs. In addition, the increased use of cancer screening tests such as chest x-ray, colonoscopy and mammogram, have reduced the impact of those devastating malignant conditions. Indeed, the use of these tests have become commonplace. Furthermore, with advancements in the treatment of acute illness such as infectious disease, and the diagnosis, treatment, and probable prevention of chronic disease, we have been blessed with better health and longevity. More importantly, the outcomes achieved by these advancements have become predictable, reproducible, and repetitive. Of course, this progress has come at a huge price tag.

We should not be surprised to find, when monetarily quantifying diagnosis and treatment, that only

10 to 25 cents of every dollar spent on medical care is physician related. While 75 to 90 cents is technology driven: such as, expenditures on medical tools and equipment associated with the diagnosis of illness, surgery interventions, and the use of pharmaceuticals. Once more, it is also unfortunate that these figures suggest a more ominous turn in the way we practice medicine today. They imply that modern medical care in our country has become synonymous with technology. This reality portends the undesirable prospect that we are slowly, and perhaps altogether, "phasing out" the involvement of our physicians in our medical care. Health Care "without physicians" is, ironically, the way medicine is being practiced in modern America. To an enormous extent, attending physicians are being replaced by paramedical nurse practitioners and medical technicians, who perform diagnostic and treatment procedures that only physicians were once licensed to do. And, our overuse of that technology has increased the overall cost of medical care.

Today's monolithic system of Health Care Organizations (HCO's), ranging from PPO's (Private Physician Organizations), HMO's (Health Management Organizations), and the more recent IPA's (Independent Physician Associations) tend to foster a manner of "health care" that is incongruous to the delivery of "quality medical care." These corporate organizations are frequently described as *vertically integrated health care systems* that can best be depicted as "top-down delivery medical care organizations."

What all vertically integrated organizations possess in common is their practice of serving populations of patients who must "choose" health care providers from *provider networks* formed by *insurance carriers* who control those networks. And to protect the profits of those insurance carriers, HCO's must strive to reduce costs by implementing "evidence-based standards-of-care." These standards, which set specific physician "rules and guidelines" that doctors are obligated to follow, often translate to lesser degrees of direct medical care and even less accountability. Under such guidelines, physicians find it difficult to behave in ways they *ought* to behave and all too easy to hide their inadequacies. In many cases, they are discouraged from consulting with other qualified physicians who are not "part of their network."

Economically speaking, Health Care in America has become a *price inelastic service*, in which medical practitioners are forced to accept whatever the insurance carriers are willing to pay for medical services. In addition, physicians in "solo practice" may be denied access to the vertically integrated health care system because other physician groups have already obtained "exclusive rights" to patient/provider contracts. Thus, the patient choice of physicians is restricted, and the result is -- more often than not -- poorer care for patients.

In addition, these organizations foster a climate of "cognitive dissonance" among physicians by requiring them to make decisions on extraneous matters: such as, the necessity to account for the legal and financial consequences of providing or withholding treatment. These distracting considerations invariably interfere with the competent physician's ability to focus on providing excellent care. These daily "states of perplexity" create dangerous situations in which doctors may underestimate their limitations and overestimate their abilities.

In a country that has the highest technological expertise for diagnosing and treating disease, and a multi-billion-dollar-a-year industry to deliver patient care, as many as 100,000 patients die every year from completely preventable physician errors. And those are just the deaths in hospitals where statistics are available. Another 100,000 patients die each year from medication errors. The fact that patients have less choice of the physician who will care for them -- physicians who know neither their patient nor their patient's medical history -- increases the likelihood of literally dying from going to a doctor. This pattern is perpetuated by passive behavior on the part of both doctors and patients. The Food and Drug Administration (FDA) reports that nearly 90% of adverse drug events go unreported by physicians, perpetuating drug-related complications for patients; and that, 75% of Americans report that they do not take their medication as directed, while 33% never fill their prescriptions at all.

While only 7% of all yearly deaths in the United States are not illness related (accidents and homicide) more than 93% of deaths *are* disease related. Of that 93%, 5% are caused by acute disease and 95% are the result of chronic disease. When evaluating the total annual cost of Health Care, expenditures for treating acute diseases are 39% and the cost of treating chronic diseases is 61%.

The overall quality of medical care in America has never been in question. This is largely attributed to the ingenuity of American scientists that continues to drive research and technological advances in the fields of medical diagnosis, surgery, and pharmacology. At the same time, the cost of federally funded Medicare and Medicaid programs (a total of $743 billion in 2010) has grown more than the costs of Social Security ($695 billion) and National Defense ($664 billion). Together, the cost of Medicare and Medicaid is second only to the combined costs of all other "discretionary" federal programs and "non-discretionary" payments on the National Debt.

When critically evaluating Health Care costs in America, two cost-drivers become apparent: acute disease and chronic disease. An acute illness presents itself as a sudden onset of symptoms. In such cases, cures are affected by the ability of a physician to effectively diagnose and treat a patient. As much as 87% of the Health Care cost of acute disease is attributed to the *clinical astuteness and knowledge of the physician.* The "father of western medicine," Hippocrates, described the attributes of clinical skill (empathy and caring, morality and altruism) more than 2,400 years ago. These attributes have been the foundation of Health Care in America since the creation of our Nation. These essential personal qualities directly translate into physician behaviors that include effective and accurate history taking, physical examination, and efficient diagnosis and treatment with minimal dependency upon laboratory tests and technology. Such actions greatly reduce medical care costs. In present-day medical schools all over the country, the attributes of caring, empathy, morality, and altruism -- as put forth by Hippocrates -- as well as the clinical skills of diagnosis and treatment are taught and cultivated. So as to mature completely throughout the career of every well trained physician. However, the present vertically integrated health care system "puts a drag" on the implementation of these physician characteristics, and instead promotes carelessness, oversight, and greed. Again, it is the *clinical astuteness and knowledge* of the physician -- or lack thereof -- that drives the cost of treatments in cases of acute illness.

In stark contrast to acute illnesses, chronic diseases are those afflictions that last a long time: at least three months or longer. Similar to acute illness, the outcome for the patient is initially influenced by the ability of the physician to effectively diagnose and treat the most common chronic illnesses such as arteriosclerotic disease and cancer. However, much less impact on a patient's chronic disease is "physician-related." As little as 12% of the cost of chronic diseases can be attributed to the clinical astuteness, skill, and knowledge of the physician. The primary goal in these medical situations is to prevent the development of chronic illness with high quality preventative health care. By engaging the motivation, proactivity, cooperation, and compliance of the patient -- to pursue long-term follow-up and preventative health measures such as routine cancer screening tests -- we can better treat predisposing subacute conditions like metabolic syndrome. Patient behavior accounts for at least 28% of the cost of chronic diseases. The impact of patient behavior is clearly an enormous factor in warding off long-term illness. No matter how well suited a doctor and their technological tools may be to the implementation of successful medical care, patient behavior is more paramount.

Health Care expenses in America can be significantly reduced by improving treatment of acute diseases by astute physicians and treatments of subacute diseases that lead to chronic disease by changing patient behavior with physician guidance through preventative medicine. Behaviors that arise in the form of cooperation, compliance, proactivity, desire and optimism are essential to -- what we the authors call -- the *triad for Health Care*. A triad that consists of *"the clinically astute physician, the best medical technology, and the motivated and proactive patient."*

But in the present-day vertically integrated health care system, there are too many players, participants, and entities calling the shots in the medical game (government, hospitals, insurance companies, physicians, and patients). Yet the simple fact is that in any good medical care system it is the skilled physician who delivers care to a willing patient. Medical care that can be provided more efficiently and cheaply without interference by "nonessential players."

It is our conviction, that Health Care in America can be improved at much reduced cost, and made more efficient and effective for both we and our posterity. We will make the case in this presentation that huge reductions in Health Care costs can be achieved by establishing and protecting a fair and free market, *horizontally integrated health care system*. A system in which Health Care in America is a *price-elastic service* in which every patient has access to every physician and the free-market determines the price of care. Where patients have "health care savings accounts" that motivate them to "shop around for the best bang for their buck," a system in which doctors provide the most cost-effective service at less cost to patients, and a system in which those individuals who consistently live healthy lifestyles are rewarded.

With that said, let us evaluate the state of Health Care in America, the mushrooming cost of that care, the dilemmas we must face to fix our current system, as well as the strategies that will make it possible to do it.

Chapter 1

"America, we have a problem."

****

Abstract

The cost of Health Care in America has gotten out of control. And despite all the party politics and media propaganda that aggravate discussions of what to do about the problem, it is we -- the American people -- who must find a way to slow those rising costs to a stand-still. As individuals in a free and democratic society, we have historically worked together to enhance the quality of life for all our citizens. And since our Founding Fathers bequeathed to us the right to *"life, liberty, and the pursuit of happiness,"* we have enjoyed unprecedented improvements in that quality of life. We have become a Nation that shares its bounty, due in part to the fact that many of the authors of the *Declaration of Independence* and our *Constitution* were scientists who welcomed and endorsed the industrial achievements of engineers and other innovative thinkers across the globe: including skilled and talented physicians who advanced the practice of medical diagnosis and discovered new ways to treat disease. Recently, however, the cost of those advances -- the development of new diagnostic and treatment technology, the capacity to more accurately diagnose and deliver proper treatments, and the business of managing and administering services to patients -- has skyrocketed. In addition, there are the mounting costs of litigating actions against medical industry providers accused of damaging the health of their patients. Together, between 1998 and 2008, these Health Care expenditures rose from $920 billion to $1.75 trillion! This is not the kind of the kind of "progress" we should to expect from our government and business sectors? There are, in fact, too many players in the game: organizations that drive up medical costs without ever getting directly involved in the medical care of patients. Instead, the achievement of excellent and affordable Health Care for all inhabitants of this country depends -- as it always has -- on the abilities of (1) well trained and knowledgeable, clinically astute and compassionate physicians, (2) scientists and engineers capable of designing and producing new medical technology, and (3) patients who are motivated and proactive in defense of their own good health to do their jobs well. Our success at solving the Health Care crisis facing America will also depend on our ability remove interlopers currently part of our Health Care system whose nonessential presence inflates the cost of care.

****

Most Americans agree that Health Care in America has become increasingly if not exorbitantly expensive. Recent estimates put the number of bankruptcies resulting from insurmountable medical expenses at more than sixty percent; and, costs continue to rise at the same time incomes of average Americans stagnate. While politicians, economists, and industry players (insurance companies) debate the multiple causes of ever-increasing Health Care costs, none of them seems able -- or at times even willing -- to help reduce those costs. It is our opinion that this failure is caused by the tendency of politicians, economists, and industry players to view the Health Care Crisis from their own political, economic, and business viewpoints. Biased perspectives that limit their capacity to find a solution to a problem that lies dangling right under their noses. It is our conclusion that government and business leaders have dropped the ball as a result of their never having laid eyes on it. However, when the practice of medicine is simplified to its most basic level -- the delivery of excellent medical care by a physician to their patient -- the solution to the problem of rising Health Care costs becomes apparent. It is the objective of this book to bring that solution to light.

Let us offer at the outset that this book is neither a dissertation on party politics nor the media hype that accompanies and exacerbates it. Nor is it a book about economic forces, nor Wall Street shenanigans, nor the impact they have on national budgets and tax-payer woes. Instead, it is a straightforward and honest analysis of a citizenry dealing with -- and attempting to solve -- health problems. It is a brief look at how we as a Nation got into this mess and how we as a Nation can get out of it. It is a book about how to renew the American Dream in the hearts and minds of our fellow citizens by focusing on the only individuals instrumental in dealing with health problems, the two individuals closest to those problems: the patient and their physician.

As individuals in a free and democratic society, we have historically worked and struggled together to enhance the quality of life for all our citizens. Since our Founding Fathers set down on parchment the basic principles that insure our freedoms -- the right to *"life, liberty, and the pursuit of happiness"* -- Americans have enjoyed unprecedented improvements in that quality of life. Since the signing of the *Declaration of Independence* in 1776 and the ratification of the *Constitution* in 1787, we have taken our people -- and the rest of the world -- on a ride that few of our forebears could have imagined. And, despite differences with our global neighbors in appearance, culture, politics, and religion we have invited the world to join our rich experience. Bequeathed the freedom to act and explore, and true to the conviction that life and individual liberty are precious, we have sought to share our advancements and substantive knowledge with the world.

It was no accident that America grew to share its bounty. Sharing is part of our creed. It is our custom to trade not only goods but also ideas. This is due in no small part to the particular circumstance that many of the authors of the *Declaration of Independence* and our *Constitution* were, in spirit and fact, scientists. They were inquisitive investigators who honored the natural philosopher's habit of inviting others to review and critique their investigations. History records that Thomas Jefferson was an acknowledged paleontologist who, like so many of his educated contemporaries, embraced the study of the natural world. The mysterious evening lights that swept over the swamps of the estate of George Washington intrigued him, and prompted him to experiment on the illumination of the curious swamp gas. And of course, there was Benjamin Franklin who is known throughout the world as one of the greatest scientists of his age. Every school child learns of his achievements in the study of the 18th Century phenomenon called "electricity." Just as it was Franklin's temper to disseminate his political views, he was quick to discuss his scientific experiments with his European colleagues: Joseph Priestley (the discoverer of oxygen) and James Watt (the inventor of a practical steam engine). These men all embraced what was then called the "natural philosophies." They neither feared nor shunned serious criticism and competition.

Our Founding Fathers' appreciation for the natural sciences stirred them to reject forms of government ruled by aristocratic relationship and whim. In a new *Age of Enlightenment*, they were driven to find a fresh brand of leaders: men and women of reason and common sense who could inspire a nation. They sought to procure a body of intelligent and compassionate government officials, enlisted by the populous, who would be responsible to a people willing to entrust those officials with the task of governing. Men like Jefferson, Washington, Adams, and Franklin strove to create a government *"... of the people, by the people, and for the people ..."* A people who cherished freedom of thought and valued the products of experimentation and innovation.

The United States of America has frequently been described as "an experiment in democracy." So it has been and still is today.

As American citizens, like our Founding Fathers, we have -- throughout our history -- tried to make a habit of practicing reason and fairness. The result has been the liberation of millions of inventive minds. The effect has been the unprecedented prospering of a nation through the free exchange of goods and ideas. Our *Constitution* made this possible by limiting the functions and powers of government officials to three restrictive tasks: *"... insure domestic tranquility, provide for the common defense, and promote the general welfare."* The *Constitution's* legacy has been the unleashing of a peoples' ingenuity. More than two centuries of inspirational creativity have led us to the development of a free economy: a system of trade that thrives on *fair* competition, invention, and the application of new and useful technology.

Within decades following the ratification of the American *Constitution*, the Industrial Revolutions in America and Europe -- the Old World having been unshackled by the New World's revolutionary example -- gathered steam. The advance of scientific technology gave the world railroads, the telegraph and telephone, the automobile and airplane. Of course, the science of mechanical engineering was not the only discipline to bestow new marvels on humankind. In both hemispheres, physicists, chemists, and biologists also contributed to the advancement of the medical arts.

In the mid-19th Century, the germ theory of the French chemist and microbiologist Louis Pasteur provided physicians with an entirely new perspective on the causes and treatment of disease. His work, and the works of thousands of other dedicated doctors and scientists here and abroad, led to the development of antiseptics, and laid the groundwork for immunology and the practice of vaccination. More than a century of research and clinical trials culminated in 1955 with the invention of the polio vaccine by the American medical researcher Jonas E. Salk. Since then, a host of new vaccines and medicinal treatments, anesthetics and analgesics, have been developed to relieve the pain and suffering of billions of Earth's inhabitants. The search for new and successful applications has continued, advancing medical technology for more than two hundred years. That progress has accelerated exponentially during the past 60 years.

Prior to the 1950's, the major focus of medical practitioners was the diagnosis and treatment of acute injury and illness. Early surgical techniques, limited medications such as penicillin and an inability to provide more long-term care, made it impossible for physicians to focus on chronic disease and chronic disease prevention. After the 1960's, however, an explosion in medical research made *preventative medicine* a reality. The diagnosis and treatment of diseases such as hypertension, hyperlipidemia, obesity, and diabetes mellitus became a major priority. When identified together in a single patient, these diseases are collectively known as *metabolic syndrome*. This physiological condition is responsible for a variety of medical disorders: including but not limited to vascular diseases of the brain (stroke), heart (heart attack), and kidney (kidney failure). In addition, cancer-screening tests (chest x-ray, colonoscopy, mammogram) have become useful and commonplace procedures. The development of new drugs have advanced the treatment of acute illnesses as well as the diagnosis and treatment of chronic diseases, making it possible for us to experience superior health and longevity of life. From 1998 to 2008, life expectancy at birth in the United States increased from 72 to 75 years for men, and 75 to 80 years for women. Despite what some in the news media and political arena would have us believe, the quality of medical care in America is quite extraordinary. Successes have become reproducible and repetitive.

Recently, however, the cost of medical care has skyrocketed. Among the causes for these mounting costs are (a) the increased cost of laboratory research required by the development of new diagnostic and treatment technology, (b) the cost of providing accurate diagnoses and delivering proper treatments, (c) the business cost of managing and administering services to patients, and (d) the cost of litigating actions against medical industry providers accused of damaging the health of those who seek their help.

Together, these costs have grown inordinately when compared to the costs of other market services. Between 1998 and 2008, Health Care expenditures -- including private health insurance costs, personal out-of-pocket expenses, Medicare (federal) and Medicaid (state) costs -- rose from $920 billion to $1.75 trillion! As a percent of our Federal Budget, the total costs of Medicare and Medicaid in 2010 superseded those of either Social Security or National Defense. After a single decade, we now pay nearly twice as much for the same level of care.

Is that kind of the kind of "progress" we can to expect from our government and business sectors? Is our journey toward a better and more democratic future about to hit a rut in the road and toss all our previous achievements into a ditch? Shall a great nation be struck gravely ill by the price of staying healthy? At what price Health Care?

Part of the problem is that, in the present-day Health Care environment, there are simply too many players in the game: players who drive up medical costs without ever lifting a finger to improve the health of patients or lessen the burdens of the physicians who treat them. As mentioned earlier, at its most basic level, matters of personal health are most important to two individuals and two individuals alone: the patient and the physician. The decisions made by these individuals, as matters of life and death, are the only decisions that matter!

Yet, in our present Health Care system, both patient and physician must constantly deal with bureaucratic institutions and individuals empowered to make decisions that have nothing to do with the well-being of patients. More often than not, these unnecessary players actually impede the prompt and proper delivery of medical services deemed appropriate by competent physicians, their interference physically and emotionally diminishing the well being of patients. Wouldn't it be smarter and economically advantageous to eliminate these superfluous players from the field of medicine?

But, there is much more to the problem of rising Health Care costs.

When critically evaluating Health Care costs in America, two major cost drivers become apparent. They are the expenses incurred by the diagnosis and treatment of *acute disease* and *chronic disease*. An acute illness or disease is a condition that presents itself suddenly -- such as appendicitis -- and is usually overcome by an intelligent physician who effectively diagnoses the condition and competently treats the patient. Costs accrued by the effective clinical supervision of patients by their physicians, in the diagnosis and treatment of acute disease, amounts to as much as 86% of the direct costs of acute medical care. As in the case of acute illness, the outcome for the patient having a chronic illness -- such as arteriosclerosis or cancer -- is initially influenced by the ability of the physician to effectively diagnose and treat the illness. However, in stark contrast to acute illness, chronic disease may take at least three months or more to develop and can afflict patients for decades. Unlike the costs of acute diseases, the direct costs of medical care attributed to the physician's effective management of chronic disease are only 12%. The responsibilities of physicians and patients with respect to the treatments and costs of acute and chronic diseases differ significantly.

Remarkably, the ancient Greek physician, Hippocrates, first categorized acute and chronic disease more than 2,400 years ago. Considered -- to this day -- to be the "father of modern medicine," Hippocrates recognized and differentiated between acute, chronic, endemic and epidemic diseases. He and his followers diagnosed and described the symptoms of dozens of familiar infirmities: such as respiratory infections, lung cancer, and heart disease. Most importantly, the great Greek identified the qualities required of any competent physician: personal attributes that could best aid that physician in diagnosing and treating illnesses. He summarized these traits in his famous *Hippocratic Oath*, the oath still taken by most every astute and knowledgeable physician: compassion and clinical skill, a sense of morality and empathy, and a personal commitment to honesty and altruism. These qualities have been the foundation of Health Care in America since its inception. Without them, the practice of good medicine is of no greater value to the soul of the body politic than the repairing of roller skates.

As they did in the time of Hippocrates, these indispensable human qualities directly translate into the physician's ability to effectively care for their patient. They make it possible for the physician to (1) ascertain through physical examination and personal interview a patient's medical history and condition, (2) accurately diagnosis and effectively treat the debilitating condition, and (3) do so with minimal dependency upon tests and technology that add unnecessarily to Health Care costs.

Of course, the primary goal of all physicians is to abort the development of chronic illness with high quality preventative health care. But in all practicality, this goal is impossible without the motivation and proactivity, co-operation and compliance of the patient. In order to best insure personal health, the patient must be vigilant in pursuing long-term follow-up and preventative health measures prescribed by their physician. Failing to do so predisposes them to subacute conditions such as metabolic syndrome. A person's dereliction of duty in advocating for their own health (by neglecting to treat hypertension, obesity and hyperlipidemia, and diabetes mellitus, or by evading routine cancer screening tests such as colonoscopy and mammography) drastically undercuts their physician's good will and treatment options. More than 28% of chronic disease cost can be attributed to patient behavior. Should we ever hope to reign in the rising cost of Health Care, that behavior must be changed.

The achievement of excellent and affordable Health Care for all inhabitants of this country is, therefore, dependent upon our willingness to nurture and reward the positive behaviors of three essential groups of individuals collectively known as the *triad for Health Care*: (1) physicians who are well trained, knowledgeable, clinically astute and compassionate, (2) scientists and engineers able to design and produce new and innovative medical technology, and (3) patients who are motivated and proactive in defense of their own good health. In addition, it will be necessary to remove interlopers currently part of the Health Care system whose nonessential presence inflates the cost of care. Any hope of reversing the trend of ever-increasing Health Care costs is doomed to fail for lack of accomplishing any of these compulsory tasks.

This is by no means an insurmountable challenge, as the people of this Nation are at their greatest in the face of adversity. And, the best of us -- proud citizens of both the past and present -- never shirked, or will ever shirk, from a challenge.

When the oxygen tank aboard the ill-fated *Apollo 13* exploded on their way to the moon, and the vacuum of outer space began to suck the life out of their craft, the astronauts aboard her didn't panic. Mission Commander, Jim Lovell, calmly reported to Mission Control: "Houston, we have a problem." Neither he nor his crew wasted a second whining or casting blame. They -- and their fellow Americans at Mission Control -- set to work solving the problems that would save the astronauts' lives.

Well, "America, we have a problem."

And, in the current political, economic, and business climates it is likely to take a revolutionary effort to save our country from bankruptcy. However, when we succeed it will surely have been a struggle that will make us worthy of the legacy left us by the men and women who founded this great country.

Having said that, it is time to take an honest and in depth look at how we got here and what we must do to confront and solve the Health Care Crisis facing America.

Chapter 2

The Hippocratic Oath and The Essence That Defines a Physician

****

Abstract

Hippocrates, the father of modern medicine, set forth the time-honored principles that should govern a proper relationship between a physician and their patient. Sadly, these codes of behavior have been "sidelined" by a system of Health Care that fails to actively support their continued observance. Being human, and through no fault of their own, the well-intentioned efforts of many good physicians have been compromised by a system in which less than competent medical practitioners can "slip through the cracks" to the detriment of patient care. Despite the enormous progress made by practitioners of the medical sciences, many of our best physicians worry that an increasing number of their colleagues, as well as too many marginally trained physician assistants, have abandoned the ideals that once graced their time-honored profession and become partly responsible for some of the problems that plague our Health Care system. They also express concern over having lost much of their authority and decision-making power with regard to their patients to third parties (government bureaucracies and health insurance companies) and the legal infrastructures that serve them. These institutions have intruded upon a decision-making process that must remain sacred and of sole concern to the physician-patient team. In addition, doctors remind us that "it takes two to tango," and that the dance performed by the physician and their patient requires not only a caring and competent healer but also the diligent considerations of the person who desires to be healthy.

****

When we are young, we think we can live forever. We take our good health for granted and challenge our bodies to keep pace with our dreams and aspirations. Until, the realities and responsibilities of adulthood glare at us from the horizon and affront our brash innocence and treasured illusions. We grow older and finally old, grateful for the waning strength we have left yet fearful that our health will fail us. Who among us cannot remember the words of an elderly aunt or uncle, grandmother or grandfather, who has blessed us with this wise affirmation: "All is well. As long as you have your health."

When we do become ill, or care for someone who is in pain, the last thing we need is distraction. We find no comfort, and have no patience, for anything -- or anyone -- that diverts us from the task of regaining our health. We don't want to think of money or having to seek financial assistance. We have little time to fill out forms, or wait in exasperation for judgments made by unfamiliar third parties having the power to decide whether or not we can "afford to be healthy" again. All we seek is the care of a kind, compassionate, and competent physician. They, and they alone, are the only people worthy of our attention and trust. In them, we see the virtues we wish we all possessed.

Physicians are our first line of defense against the enemies of health. They are obliged by their professional commitment to have a moral, ethical, and fiduciary responsibility to their patients. They have an obligation to foster the well being of their fellow conscious beings. They are the guardians of the *corpus humanus*. And, the virtues they possess -- virtues the rest of us so admire, personal traits that embody the essence that defines a physician -- lay at the core of their lifelong commitment to their craft.

To demonstrate how all Americans can have excellent and affordable Health Care, we need to examine the first essential prerequisite enumerated at the end of *Chapter 1*: that is, the education and maintenance of a skilled population of knowledgeable, clinically astute, and compassionate physicians. To do this, it is necessary to ask where -- or rather from whom -- early American physicians got their cherished ideals: ideals that to a sorry degree have been "sidelined" by many practitioners of modern American medicine. As mentioned previously, it all began in the 4th Century BCE with the father of modern medicine: Hippocrates.

Until and during the time of Hippocrates, people believed that matters of life and death could not be greatly influenced by human beings. An individual's well-being was thought to be a matter of fate, and faith and trust in the gods were favored by manifest good health. Caring for the afflicted was considered a supreme act. The citizenry of Ancient Greece elevated the deeds of those who cared for the sick and infirm to a godlike level.

Earlier civilizations had similar beliefs. In Asia dating back more than 47 centuries to 2700 BCE, Chinese officials regulating the practice of medicine also believed that the power to heal was in the hands of the gods. They called upon their revered spirits in time of need. In ancient Egypt around 2650 BCE, a physician named Imhotep -- who is credited with building the first pyramid -- was himself deified by his fellow Egyptians as "the god of healing." Even in the most advanced ancient civilizations, a person's health and well-being were thought, ultimately, to be in the hands of deities. The gods' messengers and heralds -- the physicians -- were praised as godlike. Still, matters of health were considered largely beyond the control of mortal man.

In their attempts to better serve their gods, consistent with their efforts to develop a more just and democratic society, the ancient Greeks expanded their quest to understand the world their gods had made. They embarked on a closer study of the workings of nature: including the workings of the human body.

The first Greek medical school opened in Cnidus around 700 BCE. The author of one of the earliest known works in anatomy, Alcmaeon, practiced there. Temples dedicated to Asclepius, the "healer-god," served as centers where healers diagnosed medical conditions, labored to heal the infirm, and gave medical advice along with their prognoses for recovery. At conjoining religious shrines, patients might be induced -- with the help of soporific substances such as opium -- to enter a dream-state known as *enkoimesis*. During this treatment, which was not unlike anesthesia, patients received guidance from their priests and gods. Some patients underwent invasive surgery that, not uncommonly, resulted in a cure. Healers at Asclepeia also recognized the value of better hygiene, and kept carefully controlled treatment spaces for the administration of therapies. They kept records on large marble boards, dating to 350 BCE, in which they preserved the names, complaints, case histories, and successful cures of scores of patients. Some of these surgical cures, such as the piercing of an abdominal abscess or the extraction of obviously "foreign material," were described and catalogued. It is most worthy to note that it was at Asclepeia where physicians first practiced the art and technique of observing patients and carefully examining their physical condition. It was at Asclepeia where ancient Greeks physicians developed one of the first theoretical explanations of the causes of illness: humoral theory.

According to this theory, illness developed as the result of an imbalance of the body humors. These bodily fluids -- discovered in the course of anatomical investigations made on meticulously dissected cadavers -- included black bile originating in the spleen, yellow bile dispensed by the gall bladder, phlegm exuded by the brain and lungs, and blood produced by the liver. The physicians of Asclepeia, including Hippocrates, believed that afflictions of these organs were the result of an imbalance of the humors. In addition, these ancient Greeks surmised that the particular balance of the bodily humors in any individual determined that person's personality traits and dispositions. To this day, someone who is calm, sluggish, or apathetic may be described as "phlegmatic." So as a matter of simple logic, the goal of every ancient Greek physician was to keep the body's humors in balance. In Hippocrates' efforts to achieve this goal, and thereby alleviate some of the discomfort and anxiety of his patients, the great Greek personally manifested a compassionate bedside manner that he deemed necessary to the practice of his art.

In a collection of volumes known as the *Hippocratic Corpus*, the empirical discoveries and reflections of Hippocrates were recorded for posterity. This body of work included seventy medical texts. In his greatest work, Hippocrates inscribed his deliberations on what he considered to be the obligatory duties and personal qualities of every good physician. In just eight short paragraphs, Hippocrates set forth these obligations and individual attributes in an oath. That oath -- until it was replaced in 1964 by a modern version deemed "better suited" to the times -- became the guiding opus shared by every American physician. The universal, ethical, social, and economic values set forth in the original *Hippocratic Oath* are rich and complex. Together, these values -- which embody the essence that defines a physician -- serve as the most important key to unlocking the door that bars our way to the solution to America's Health Care Crisis. Adherence to the values laid out by Hippocrates can serve to hasten our achieving the goal of excellent and inexpensive Health Care for all.

Read the following translation of the original *Hippocratic Oath* and reflect upon an America that has lost its way.

The Classical Version of The Hippocratic Oath

I swear by Apollo Physician and Asclepius and Hygieia and Panaceia and all the gods and goddesses, making them my witnesses, that I will fulfill according to my ability and judgment this oath and this covenant:

To hold him who has taught me this art as equal to my parents and to live my life in partnership with him, and if he is in need of money to give him a share of mine, and to regard his offspring as equal to my brothers in male lineage and to teach them this art -- if they desire to learn it -- without fee and covenant; to give a share of precepts and oral instruction and all the other learning to my sons and to the sons of him who has instructed me and to pupils who have signed the covenant and have taken an oath according to the medical law, but no one else.

I will apply dietetic measures for the benefit of the sick according to my ability and judgment; I will keep them from harm and injustice.

I will neither give a deadly drug to anybody who asked for it, nor will I make a suggestion to this effect. Similarly, I will not give to a woman an abortive remedy. In purity and holiness I will guard my life and my art.

I will not use the knife, not even on sufferers from stone, but will withdraw in favor of such men as are engaged in this work.

Whatever houses I may visit, I will come for the benefit of the sick, remaining free of all intentional injustice, of all mischief and in particular of sexual relations with both female and male persons, be they free or slaves.

What I may see or hear in the course of the treatment or even outside of the treatment in regard to the life of men, which on no account one must spread abroad, I will keep to myself, holding such things shameful to be spoken about.

If I fulfill this oath and do not violate it, may it be granted to me to enjoy life and art, being honored with fame among all men for all time to come: If I transgress it and swear falsely, may the opposite of all this be my lot.

The spirit of the *Hippocratic Oath* is just as germane today as it was at the founding of our Republic. In the Oath, every physician swears to honor in partnership the mentors who taught him/her the skills required of a medical practitioner. They swear to give of themselves -- without primary regard to monetary considerations -- all they have learned of their art. They vow to apply their knowledge, to the best of their ability, for the benefit of the sick in an effort to protect them from harm and the ill treatment by others. A modern physician today may adhere to the oath by swearing to counsel those contemplating suicide or abortion and to withhold such treatments that run contrary to the well-being of such individuals. They would pledge to never invade the integrity of the human body in any way unless the life of the patient is threatened or put at unreasonable risk. They would promise to respect the people whose homes they visit, in pursuit of making them well, and refrain from all distracting mischief. They would swear to keep to themselves what they see or hear in the course of treating the weak and infirm, and to respect the confidentiality of all those they serve. And, should they fail to abide by the Oath, they would vow to accept just punishments due them to the same degree they would have favored reward for having fulfilled it.

For centuries following the death of Hippocrates in 377 BCE, until the Dark and Middle Ages when laws of reason were abandoned in favor of irrational superstition, physicians abided by his precepts. It wasn't until the start of the *Enlightenment* in the 18th and 19th Centuries that those precepts were, once again, discovered and adopted in high regard. Yet, during the American Revolution -- despite the good will and true intentions of many an able healer -- colonial physicians still had little influence over the frailties of life and portents of death.

Viewed as a cooperative effort among dedicated individuals who serve the needs of the sick, Health Care is not even mentioned in the *Constitution*. The idea was nonexistent in the 18th Century. For lack of proper knowledge and an efficient "physician's infrastructure," George Washington died of a simple sore throat that flared into an infectious peritonsilar abscess. Over the next two centuries, diagnosis and patient care as well as medical advancements and treatment were made ever so slowly. Nevertheless, small advances were the direct result of creative and tedious scientific research that continues unabated to modern times.

During the 19th Century, Joseph Lister and Louis Pasteur spoke and published about bacterial infections, antiseptics, and vaccination. In the 1940's, Alexander Fleming developed penicillin, and Alfred Blalock did the first heart surgery. In the 1950's, Jonas Salk developed the vaccine for polio that most Baby Boomers remember receiving. The ability to successfully diagnose and treat patients is still evolving. And, consistent with the oath they took as graduating medical students, physicians of that time ascribed to Hippocrates' edict to "do no harm."

At the middle of the 20th Century, physicians often felt exuberant about their ability to not only tend and care for their patients but also to treat and heal. During that time being a doctor felt good. And, for the most part, being a patient wasn't much of a horror either: nor was the price of competent medical care.

Most Baby Boomers can recall the first medical dramatizations on television. They may remember a TV show called *Medic*, starring Richard Boone. His opening statement for every episode, described his character as possessing the "Eye of an Eagle," the "Heart of a Lion," and the "Hand of a Woman:" traits that still ring true today for many a physician. Those of us, who grew up in that era, still retain an enduring image of a doctor as a caring person, a dependable friend, who would leave their own family to come out at night to help their fellow man. Whether or not we could pay for that help. *Medic* was followed by other riveting medical series which also portrayed doctors as caring, moral, and trustworthy people who did their very best to help others: many times at risk to their own life and well being. *Ben Casey*, *Doctor Kildare* and *Marcus Welby, MD* was there to lend a helping hand. And later, in their efforts to demonstrate that the time-honored qualities of a physician were gender neutral, Hollywood gave us *Dr. Quinn, Medicine Woman*. These television shows were spellbinding for viewers and, at the same time, emphasized the relationship between a truly caring and compassionate doctor and their patient. That patient, in return, showed an honest respect and admiration for the healer who cared for them. There was no questioning: "Who is in charge?" Clearly, the physician and patient were a team: a team dedicated to pursuing the optimum healing and longevity of the individual patient.

In the 1970's, '80s, and '90s, viewers were glued to *MASH*, *St. Elsewhere*, *ER*, and *House*. These teleplays dramatized many of the personal complexities and sacrifices made by modern physicians. As in days gone by, today's physicians experience long working hours, marital stress, lost relationships, the pain of losing patients, as well as the distress of ethical conflicts surrounding organ transplants and the withdrawal of care from the terminally ill. For their sacrifice, the general public came to appreciate doctors all the more.

What has changed? How are things different today? How is it that, at the turn of the 21st Century, we have become so increasingly preoccupied and concerned with issues concerning Health Care in our society? Why has Health Care suddenly become a major problem demanding our immediate and interminable attention? Who if anyone is at fault? Who is in charge?

In times of crisis, it is natural to be drawn to an examination of the causes that may, or may not have, precipitated that crisis. Most unfortunately, it is also not uncommon for us to look for someone to blame.

Some find it all too easy to place the blame for the Health Care Crisis on physicians. They may argue that medical practitioners, today, less commonly invoke the *Hippocratic Oath*? They find it fortuitous to suggest that physicians of a new generation have lost their bedside manner. They ask: "Has their lust for gold become more important to them than the Golden Rule?"

Perhaps, the propensity to blame physicians for being part of what ails our Health Care system derives from our habit of expecting so much of them. Despite the advance of history and the transformations of culture since the days of Hippocrates, we still tend to revere our doctors as though they were gods. So, as social systems become more complex and, at times, unwieldy, we put the blame on those we imagine to be the most able, the smartest and most intelligent among us, for having failed to solve the problems that afflict us.

How dare they value gold above the Golden Rule! What kind of people are they? They're smart. That's for sure. Why don't they use that intelligence to get us out of this mess?

Many of us seem to feel that someone who is very smart is -- by definition -- gifted or some kind of genius. Each of us can name many exceptional individuals whom we consider blessed with extraordinary gifts and abilities: Albert Einstein and Stephen Hawking, Mozart and Beethoven, Michelangelo and Picasso, Thomas Jefferson and Benjamin Franklin, or Steve Jobs and Bill Gates. Gifted individuals abound in the sciences, the arts, and -- yes -- in the arenas of politics and business. However, when the skills and talents of these individuals are examined more closely, we usually find them to be lacking other admirable human traits, the lack of which only lessens our opinion of them. We begin to realize that intelligence is not one-dimensional. It is multifaceted and can be expressed in many different ways. The brain of an individual we consider "intelligent" may not make him as much of a "genius" as we might think.

To make use of a metaphor: While a home may be a wonderfully congenial, beautifully flowing, tastefully and sagaciously decorated domicile, the "rooms" (the structures and functions) of the human brain have been lumped together by the serendipitous forces of biological mutation and natural selection. The organ is not the product of careful and painstaking architectural planning. Instead, this amazing hunk of flesh -- that houses the essence of who we are -- was put together in a most happenstance way. It can be more accurately likened to a lodging with many different and sometimes incongruent rooms. Most of us have brains that could be described as having a most delightful living room, but a blasé den, and a master bathroom with questionable plumbing. The living room gets an "A-rating," while the den is rated "C" and the bathroom an ignominious "F." After all, nobody is perfect. On careful examination, we would in all probability conclude that no gifted intellect gracing the pages of history was a perfect genius.

Yet somehow, we expect our physicians to be just that!

After all, they are the healers. They are the gods' heralds. They are the guardians of the corpus humanus. So, in addition to their intellect, they must also embody and manifest the most valued of all human traits: competency, compassion, common decency, common sense, and a quintessential moral compass. We desire them to be some kind of large imposing residence, welcoming all humanity to its door, with every room earning straight "AAA-ratings" and more. It is not enough for a physician to be a "gifted intellect." They must also be a singularly, special human being. They must be a true genius *par excellence*!

But is that humanly possible?

The physician who earned straight A's in medical school is undoubtedly brilliant and has a strong overall knowledge base. But, their accomplishments as a medical student say little about their personal and profession attitudes, their conscientiousness, their sense of morality, or their clinical talents for recognizing what's wrong with a patient which, in turn, gives rise to their capacity to implement creative and on-the-spot therapeutic strategies. Too often, to the detriment of patient care, physicians who are plenty smart, intellectually and technologically, are unable to figure out what is wrong with a patient. And more sadly -- in our modern day vertically integrated health care system -- they might not even care.

There is an old riddle: "What do you call a doctor who earned all "D's" in medical school?" Answer: "You call them 'Doctor.'"

As in any vocation or profession, there are good and bad practitioners. Bad physicians, like fumbling auto mechanics, unimpressive teachers, and greedy banking executives cost the taxpayer millions, if not billions, of dollars a year. In the field of Health Care, the actions of poor and unfeeling physicians provide us with substandard care. In a system that would -- were it otherwise -- be more than capable of providing the best Health Care in the world! In concrete terms, this financial calamity is exacerbated when indecisive doctors find that they need to substitute excessive lab tests and imaging studies for analytical thought, sound judgment, and well considered and prudent diagnoses. When physicians are unsure, and unable to deal with their uncertainty *by stopping to focus and think*, they tend to panic, and "shotgun" every test they can until they land on a plausible and -- dare we say it -- billable answer. In these cases, whether or not the patient improves becomes a secondary matter.

Ultimately, what America's Health Care system needs are doctors who embody all the Hippocratic virtues of being a physician (kindness, intuition, empathy for humankind, an unwavering morality) and an adequate intellect that supplements those virtues with clinical astuteness aided by technical knowledge. Of course, their natural abilities and hard-won skills -- in any fair and equitable capitalist economy such as the one the Founding Fathers wished for their fledgling nation -- deserve to be fairly compensated.

It is our observation that the virtues possessed by the vast majority of America's physicians -- values that lay at the core of their lifelong commitment to their craft -- are still with them. Most have chosen to live and work adhering to the precepts of the *Hippo-cratic Oath* while others have not. It is one of the goals of this book, to provide a plan that will help to further aggrandize the medical profession by insuring that individuals who lack these virtues and skills never become -- or ever remain -- licensed physicians in America.

Most every physician will admit that many of their colleagues, and too many marginally trained physician assistants, are partly to blame for some of the problems that plague our Health Care system. They will also express concern over having lost much of their authority and decision-making power -- with regard to their patients -- to third parties (government bureaucrats and health insurance company employees and the legal infrastructures that serves them). These parties intrude upon a decision-making process that ought to be the sole concern of the physician-patient team. As will be discussed in *Chapter 4*, doctors also remind us "it takes two to tango." And that, the dance performed by a physician and their patient requires, not only a caring and competent healer, but also the diligent considerations of the person who desires to stay well.

But, before we turn our attention to that most crucial relationship -- and how to improve it -- we need to consider the role played by those who provide America with new and more innovative medical tech-nology: devices that expand the diagnostic and thera-peutic strategies employed by competent healers.

Chapter 3

Good Science and Technology Are
The Foundations of Good Medicine But Not Its Soul

****

Abstract

The accelerating rapidity of advancements made in the field of medicine stems, in good part, from an explosion of information in a host of scientific disciplines. This information has made possible the development of new technologies that have blended with knowledge in the art and practice of clinically astute medicine. The maintenance of a task force of scientists and engineers, able to design and produce new, innovative, and less expensive medical technology, is an essential requisite for solving the Health Care Crisis. Yet, while good science and technology are the foundations of good medicine, they are not its soul. At the heart of the practice of medicine is the heart of the physician: a caring and compassionate, clinically astute and experienced doctor who knows when the best technology at their disposal can do more harm than good.

****

While America must surely maintain an army of knowledgeable, clinically astute and compassionate physicians, that achievement alone would not prove sufficient in our efforts to provide all Americans with excellent and affordable Health Care. While we expect our doctors to manifest a country-doctor-demeanor and caring disposition, consistent with the tenets of the *Hippocratic Oath*, we must also demand that they make competent use of ever-evolving computer-state-of-the-art technology.

The accelerating pace of change in medicine stems from an explosion of scientific information, resulting in the constant development of new technology, and the need to blend that information into the art and practice of clinically astute medicine. The maintenance of a task force of scientists and engineers, able to design and produce new and innovative medical technology, is the second essential requisite for solving the Health Care Crisis.

Compared to the virtually sterile surgical rooms available to the average American patient, today, the treatment spaces set aside by the healers at Cnidis in Ancient Greece were a dump. By modern standards, the crude tools used by these early physicians also left much to be desired. In addition, ancient healers commonly failed to clean -- let alone sterilize -- their surgical tools. Louis Pasteur, the discoverer of germ theory, would not be born for nearly two more millennium. In fact, until the late 19th Century, most doctors didn't bother to wash their hands before examining a patient or performing an operation.

The role of science in medicine is clear. Science-based technology -- the product of careful deductive reasoning and painstaking experimentation -- forms the foundation for the solution to many clinical problems. Over little more than a century, astonishing advances in physics and the materials sciences have resulted in the invention of more powerful microscopes and imaging techniques. These instruments have allowed physicians, and their laboratory assistants, to examine the most miniature parts of the body. These devices have made possible the visualization of individual cells and the tiny organelle components that comprise those miraculous living entities. Today, physicians have at their disposal such device-dependent diagnostic procedures as x-ray, ultrasound, electrocardiograms (EKG) and electroencephalograms (EEG), magnetic resonance imagining (MRI), positron emission tomography (PET) and computerized axial tomography (CAT) scans. These procedures give physicians the opportunity to view the workings of internal organs in real time.

Advances in cell biology, molecular biology, biochemistry, and genetics have opened avenues of investigation that have resulted in the formulation of new theories to explain the pathological physiology (pathophysiology) of disease and the disease process as it effects healthy human tissues, organs, and organ systems. These insights have led to a better understanding of complex disease processes and driven medical researchers toward new approaches to disease diagnosis, treatment, and illness prevention. They have also led to the discovery of vaccines that have been remarkably and routinely successful in preventing the contraction and spread of diseases: cholera (1879), rabies (1885), tetanus (1890), typhoid fever (1896), bubonic plague (1897), tuberculosis (1927), yellow fever (1932), influenza (1945) polio (1952), measles (1963), mumps (1967), rubella (1970), chicken pox (1974), pneumonia (1977), and the list goes on and on. In particular, the sciences of biology and chemistry have branched off into the subdisciplines of biochemistry and its daughter discipline *pharmacology*.

Pharmacology is the study of both natural and synthetic chemical substances and the examination of how they interact with the cells and tissues of living organisms. Early pharmacologists of the 19th Century focused their attention mainly on natural substances such as plant extracts. However, scientific progress in 20th Century chemistry -- particularly advances in the study of hydrocarbons (chemicals found in crude oil) have made the development of many useful synthetic substances possible. Any substance found to have healthy medicinal value is called a *pharmaceutical*.

The study of pharmacology includes the examination of a drug's molecular structure, its physical and chemical properties, and its physiological -- both medicinal and toxic -- interactions with living tissues. Pharmacologists study how drugs are absorbed, distributed, processed and excreted from biological systems. Only after pharmacologists are finished developing and testing a particular medicine -- a complex and costly process -- is that medication offered to the general public. Pharmacists then take over the biomedical process of preparing and dispensing medicine to patients at the correct dosage and with appropriate directions for their use.

As will be discussed in *Chapter 6*, all of these scientific and technological advances in the art and science of medical care do not come without substantial cost and investment.

Needless to say, America will need to educate and employ battalions of citizens both motivated and skilled at inventing new drugs and diagnostic technology. It will largely be the responsibility of our professional educators from kindergarten to university -- in concert with our best scientists, engineers, and physicians -- to succeed in graduating these dedicated innovators. It will be the responsibility to all of us to insure that a free and fair market economy amply rewards those individuals and firms who provide us with the best and least expensive medical technology. Recent studies comparing our country with that of other industrial democracies have shown that we are seriously behind in that endeavor.

A recent article in *Scientific American* grieved over the fact that too many of America's intelligent and talented youth, are opting out of the sciences and choosing other professions that currently pay better salaries. Firms all over the country are experiencing a shortage of graduates in the so-called STEM disciplines (science, technology, engineering, and math). While more women entering college are being awarded more science degrees, there is a shortfall in the overall number of competent students choosing science and engineering professions. Despite the fact that the number of job openings and graduates are about the same, salaries earned in "less demanding" business and management professions are more appealing. Graduates are drawn to professions that grant them greater status and less responsibility. Much of this behavior can be attributed to the fact that the cost of a higher education in the STEM disciplines -- much like that in the field of medicine -- has become excessive. It is a simple matter of economics for students to view business degrees as the best bet toward finding a job that will help pay off their student loans. There is also concern that less than competitive salaries offered by many firms in the business of developing new medical products result from their organizations spending more on advertising their products (drug ads by pharmaceutical firms) than they do in developing them.

Nevertheless, highly advanced diagnostic and therapeutic technology and procedures are a major part of the practice of medicine and its availability for use must remain everpresent. Yet, being skillful in the most sophisticated applications of this diagnostic and therapeutic technology -- alone -- does not guarantee that our "healers" will make the best physicians and that patient health outcomes will always be positive. All too often, it is more clinically astute to use less technology rather than more.

When a physician is presented with a patient's challenging clinical problems, they face the difficult job of identifying the pertinent signs and symptoms manifested by the patient's discomfort. All this must be done within the context of that patient's complex medical history. It is the goal of the doctor's physical examination to extract the crucial laboratory and test data -- from relevant test results -- to determine whether "to treat" or "not to treat." The Hippocratic directive to "do no harm" must be of conspicuous consideration to the physician. Deciding whether or not the clinical clues found during a disease-history evaluation, physical diagnosis, and essential series of laboratory tests using the latest technology are worth pursuing are all relevant to the clinically astute decision-making process employed by the physician. After which, the doctor must weigh whether or not a proposed treatment entails greater risk than the disease itself. These are judgments that every skilled clinician must make many times a day!

The truly astute physician pursues two simultaneous courses: (1) an ongoing search for more definitive clues (signs and symptoms), which (2) leads to the generation and selection of concrete hypotheses (diagnoses). The evaluation of signs and symptoms, followed by diagnosis, begin almost simultaneously with the first contact between the patient and the clinically astute physician. This combination of comprehensive medical knowledge, applicable experience, sound judgment and intuition defines the "art of medicine." These skills constitute what amounts to a physician's *clinical astuteness*. They are as essential to the practice of medicine as state-of-the-art technology (x-ray, ultrasound, CAT scan, MRI, etc.) and evidence-based medicine (scientific research and standardized professional guidelines, etc.). Without them, a doctor is incapable of recognizing the clues needed to prescribe a cure for what ails their patient.

It has certainly been the case that the advancement of technology, including laboratory and special anatomic and physiologic examinations, has been remarkable during the past 30 years. Such progress has been of enormous value to the modern healer in the screening and diagnosing of disease processes. However, with their ease of availability, and the *presumed absolute accuracy* of this wide array of technologies, there has evolved a drawback. In recent years, an enormous reliance on these investigative tools and their roll in helping to find solutions to clinical problems has grown along with an unwarranted and, at times, unrealistic confidence in them.

The unquestionable confidence that many doctors have for this remarkable technology often promotes an arbitrary decision -- many times based *solely* on the interpretation of test results -- as to whether or not a disease process is actually present. This growing, and at times shameful, approach to examining patients -- which can precipitate the *over-utilization of technology* -- often dramatically affects the ability to diagnose. This, in turn, affects the choice of selected treatments and frequently short-changes patients. Furthermore, problematic patients seen in office and out-patient settings, and in emergency room and hospital settings, are routinely referred for imaging and other tests with no or minimal hands-on history or physical examination. This increasingly more prevalent "hands-off" approach defies the traditionally accepted medical doctrine: *"When in doubt look at the patient."*

The habit-forming dependence on diagnostic technology has given many a physician blinders and tunnel vision. It has, one could surmise, caused many a doctor lacking a sensitive bedside manner to conclude that a blow to the shoulder that doesn't turn red must not hurt! A truly clinically astute physician -- one who compassionately notes the grimace of pain on their patient's face -- perceives, ponders, congers and feels their way toward an appropriate diagnosis and effective treatment with minimal intervention of otherwise unnecessary technology.

The level of expertise of a physician, which includes thorough training, comprehensive knowledge, experience, and *time devoted to the patient's problem*, is the most important factor in determining the effectiveness and rapidity of diagnosis and treatment. In many cases, a clinically astute physician can identify a disease process almost at a glance, prior to the implementation of a clinical "work up (investigation of patient history, physical examination, and relevant testing). Such "snap diagnosis" are described by two German words: *augenblick*, meaning "eye moment," and *gestaltung*, meaning "configuration or condition." The ability to make an accurate *augenblick gestaltung* can hasten treatment, thereby reducing medical costs with efficient clinical care. The search for clues and the generation of selected hypotheses that lead to useful diagnoses requires the intelligent use of four separate but sequentially integrated strategies: (1) the consideration of patient medical history and symptoms, (2) careful and thorough hands-on physical examination manifested with clinical astuteness, (3) *appropriate* laboratory tests, and (4) *suitable* anatomic and physiologic examinations.

All physicians have had patients for whom imaging and other diagnostic tests have found abnormalities leading to unexpected diagnoses. Nonetheless, too many patients have been asked to endure too many tests and needless exams that add unnecessary costs to the cause of providing excellent Health Care. Redundant and even superfluous testing has become one of the major cost-drivers of our present system of Health Care. A clinically astute physician knows how to use diagnostic tools judiciously. They know how to ask, on a consistent basis, whether or not the results of such tests will alter treatment management for the benefit of the patient. The practice of medicine is an art based on science. It is learned at the bedside and not in the classroom.

Indeed, good science and technology are the foundations of good medicine. But they are not its soul. At the heart of the practice of medicine is the heart of the physician: a caring and compassionate, clinically astute and experienced doctor who knows when even the best technology at their disposal may do more harm than good.

Still, the best efforts of the most skilled healers, making appropriate use of the most effective medicines and advanced medical technology, would be for naught without the considerate cooperation of a population of mindful, proactive and obliging patients. Without that cooperation the solution to the Health Care Crisis facing America will forever elude us.

Chapter 4

Being A Patient Requires More Than
Just Being Patient

****

Abstract

As much as the physician who cares for us, it is we -- as individuals -- who bear ultimate responsibility for maximizing our own well being by acting proactively in defense of our own good health. Unfortunately, too many of us have reneged on our unwritten contract with our fellow Americans by making it harder for our government leaders to *"... promote the general welfare."* Those who behave irresponsibly by failing to follow the simplest instructions of their doctors -- regarding their advice to get vaccinated against preventable illnesses, eat a proper diet, exercise daily, and avoid the abusive ills of tobacco and excessive alcohol -- are costing us hundreds of billions of dollars per year. Yet, by what right, do we presume to infringe on the rights of others and tell them how they must behave? Is it possible to create a fair and equitable system that will provide Health Care for all while continuing to preserve our freedom of choice and individual liberties? How can the additional, personal economic burden in taxes and insurance premiums placed on those who already live healthy lifestyles -- monies supporting those who cause us to spend too much on Health Care -- be ameliorated? And, how are we to motivate those who live unhealthy lifestyles to change their behavior? To do this, it will be necessary to provide every American with a fair and equitable financial incentive that accrues monetary benefits to those proactive individuals who make the maintenance of their personal health a priority and matter of routine. Creating a truly fair and free market for Health Care services, where both physician and patients stand to gain from a fair and evenhanded exchange, will make it possible for individuals to be re-educated on how to behave proactively in defense of their own good health and become inspired and motivated to do so. Giving all of us the financial incentive to live healthier lives, will lead to better long-term health and the personal enjoyment and satisfaction that comes with the regular practice of healthful behaviors. At the same time, these measures will lead to significant reductions in Health Care costs.

****

Let us assume for a moment that America succeeds in producing and maintaining "a skilled population of knowledgeable, clinically astute, and compassionate physicians." And, that our educational system manages to graduate an army of superb biologists, chemists and engineers able to conceive, design, and manufacture the pharmaceuticals and diagnostic machinery and surgical apparatus required by legions of competent physicians. Shall we have succeeded in reigning in the exorbitant cost of Health Care in America? Will the optimal solution to the current Health Care Crisis have been found?

Consider the following patient.

"Help me, Doctor! Help me! Yes, I know I smoke and drink too much. I know I am overweight. I know I haven't exercised as much as I should. And, I haven't been taking those pills you gave me because they make me feel funny. But, this high blood pressure, diabetes, and high cholesterol are killing me. You're the doctor! It's your job to save me!"

The average American physician is likely to report that the individual exemplified above is not an altogether fictional character. They show up in doctor's offices and in hospital emergency rooms every day.

With a single glance at the number of obese shoppers, both young and old, frequenting the supermarkets of America, today, one is tempted to argue that our fellow citizens have simply forgotten how to take care of themselves. This has incited many a taxpayer to voice the opinion that they should not have to pay for the medical care of those who do little or nothing to maintain their own good health. While we gain little by casting blame on others, the very real and disturbing fact remains that there are too many among us who mistreat their bodies. They smoke too much, drink too much, rarely exercise, and gorge on a diet that is unbalanced or altogether void of essential nutrients.

To what extent should these individuals be held accountable for driving up Health Care costs? To what extent does any of us have the legal right to dictate the personal habits of others by telling them what they should eat, what they can drink, and what they may inhale. If John Doe wants to smoke a daily pack of cigarettes -- despite the fact that the best medical research has shown conclusively that cigarette smoking damages vital organs -- then who are we to tell him he can't. And, who among us would want our taxes raised in order to pay for the tools and manpower the government would need to enforce such legal restrictions. To what extent does any of us have the moral right to tell anyone else how they must live?

Since the days of our Founding Fathers, Americans have always cherished and defended their individual liberties; and, government representatives that make laws that inadvertently (or by design) restrict those liberties do so at their political peril. Is it possible -- in a nation that has, so far, thrived on a fair and free market economy -- for us to create a cost-effective, efficient, and compassionate Health Care system that manages to *stay in the black* without restricting individual liberty. No matter how foolhardy the "liberties" taken by the risk-takers among us happen to be?

There is no doubt that individuals who live an un-healthy life style -- according to the best medical and economic assessments -- increase Health Care costs. All of our available knowledge -- concerning diagnosis and treatment of diseases and the application of preventative medicine with regard to nutrition, medication, and diagnostic investigation -- is lost on the person who, for whatever reason, cares little about, and fails to take responsibility for, their own health. Until they wind up in the emergency room.

Whereas, patients who respect and contribute to the physician-patient relationship -- by taking responsibility for their own well-being -- cost the Health Care system considerably less. Individuals who are proactive in defense of their own good health make a sincere effort to communicate with their doctor and his/her office staff. They are punctual to medical appointments, complete their physician's ordered tests and treatments in a timely fashion, and take appropriate medications designed to prevent future disorders. These individuals suffer fewer and less serious illnesses.

It is reassuring that the vast majority of Americans have become aware of medical care issues to the extent that such concerns have become familiar to most of us. They are often the topic of conversation. Many of us have heard comments like the following: "Sorry. I won't be able to play golf on Monday, because I'm scheduled to have my colonoscopy, or my mammogram, or my Pap smear that morning."

Furthermore, we have become more knowledgeable regarding specific subacute medical conditions that can seriously and even fatally threaten our future health: such as metabolic syndrome. Most of us are already personally aware that we can take specific actions that will help to improve our own health in this regard. We can make sure to get an adequate amount of sleep, stop smoking, decrease our alcohol intake, exercise in concordance with our age and overall physical condition, and make sure we get proper nutrition. The burden of responsibility for taking each of these actions -- which can achieve maximum health benefits that will have a direct impact on our daily lives -- falls directly upon the shoulders of the individual patient.

There is also good reason to suspect and hope, thanks to the Internet, that present and future generations of Americans are -- and will be -- better informed than previous generations concerning available Health Care and the field of Preventative Medicine. Yet, any statistician will remind us that the range of behaviors of any population of individuals takes the shape of a *normal curve*: a distribution that includes poor performers, fair performers, average performers, better than average performers, and the best performers. Despite increases in the number for average, better, and best performers, there will always be poor and fair performers within any population.

Faced with the reality that not all human beings will act responsibly, even when the chips are down, we find it necessary to ask the following question: Is it possible to create a democratically viable Health Care system that can provide excellent and inexpensive medical care for all in a fair and equitable way?

We, the authors, are as confident as the men and women who gave birth to this great Nation that it is. But, to demonstrate how it is possible, we need to examine the facts. Let us consider, for a moment, a few of the basic statistics on the leading causes of death in the United States.

FIGURE 1

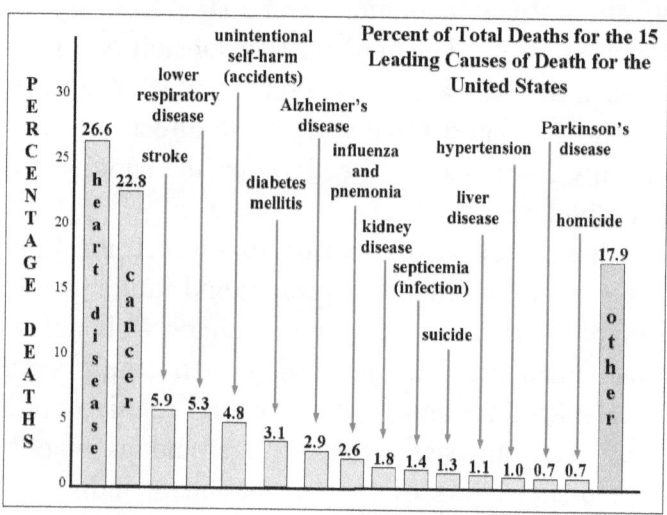

FIGURE 1 above is taken from a report of a lengthy study conducted from 2005-2006 by the *Cen-*

ters for Disease Control and Prevention (CDC)/ National Center for Health Statistics (NCHS)/ National Vital Statistics System (NVSS).

Despite dramatic media coverage of deaths by acts of violence (homicides, suicides, and unintentional self-harm such as car accidents), it is clear that -- of the fifteen leading causes of death in the United States of America -- twelve are disease-related. This accounts for about 93.2% of those deaths. Only 6.8% of the deaths are caused by acts of violence (homicides, suicides, and unintentional self-harm such as airplane disasters). Of those diseases that are disease-related about 35% are atherosclerotic or cardiovascular related diseases caused by clogged arteries: including heart disease (26.6%), stroke (cerebrovascular disease: 5.9%), renal vascular disease (kidney disease: 1.8%), and hypertension (high blood pressure: 1.0%). About 22.8% of all deaths are cancer related. Of which, as reported in the same study, more than 90% are cancers of the lung, colon, breast, liver, cervix, prostate, mouth, throat, and esophagus.

Trillions of dollars are spent annually for medication, chemotherapy, surgery (curative and palliative resection, vascular, reconstructive, transplant, etc.), and radiation for the treatment of atherosclerotic and cancer related diseases. These procedures are performed not only in the early stages of a disease but also when cases become terminal.

According to the same study, from 25 to 40% of the money currently spent on Health Care for the average American is expended during the last 5 to 10 years of life. There is no doubt that national Health

Care expenditures could be drastically reduced by the comprehensive treatment of acute disease -- by perhaps as much as 50 to 60% -- by maximizing the *clinical astuteness of all physicians* and by promoting the *proactive cooperation of all patients* in an effort to stop subacute diseases from developing into chronic disease. Both the doctor and their patient must nurture and reinforce an *attitude that changes patient behavior through preventative medicine.*

How can this be accomplished?

The current vertically integrated system of Health Care has surely failed to do it. One likely reason is that patients, once insured, may take their health for granted. Expecting that they will be cared for and cured at the onset of debilitating illnesses. With faith in this conviction, many of our fellow citizens have lost the incentive to take responsibility for their own and their children's health: a situation that costs *all of us* many hundreds of billions of dollars a year.

Preventative medicine (behavior dominated by actions most immediately taken by the patient) is now supported by most health insurance plans. Of course, the primary motive of these business institutions is to increase their profits by spending less on chronic disease care. These companies have promoted preventative medicine by encouraging their customers to seek out colonoscopies, antihypertensive and antihyperlidemia medication, vaccinations, and a multitude of other diagnostic blood, imaging and endoscopic tests. All of these exams are, of course, able to detect diseases before they become too costly to treat for both the insurer and, consequently, the insured. Thus, insurance companies -- whose sole purpose in the free market is to make money by becoming the "middleman" between the doctor and their patient (a rather un-Hippocratic thing to do) -- find their profits threatened when patients do not take responsibility for their own good health. It is this consideration, alone, that prompted the birth of corporate medical conglomerates formed to "teach people how to maintain good health." These organizations became known as *health maintenance organizations*: HMO's. In *Chapter 6*, we will discuss the impact that these corporations have had on the delivery and expense of Health Care in America.

Regardless of the kind of health insurance policy a person has, or does not have, one would think they would be thrilled to find relatively painless and convenient, safe and accurate medical tests that help doctors to diagnose and prevent the onset of chronic disease in their earliest stages of development. However, patient compliance with doctor's orders has actually been dismal. Obvious reasons for poor compliance include (1) lack of information, (2) low priority and lack of time given the day-to-day struggle to earn a living, and (3) simply not caring.

The examples presented below illustrate how lacking patient participation has been -- with regard to taking proactive screening and preventative Health Care measures (cancer screening, vaccination, etc.) -- in combating subacute diseases that lead to chronic disease.

Example #1: Failure to Screen for Cancer.

Colon cancer, the second leading cause of cancer death in the United States (56,300 per year), arises as a projection of glandular tissue called an *adenomatous polyp*: a polyp that can easily be removed as part of the colonoscopy procedure. If guidelines set by the *American Gastroenterological Association* (AGA) were vigorously followed, colonoscopy would almost totally eliminate the 130,200 new colon cancer cases physicians diagnose every year. Those guidelines direct doctors to advise their patients to have a colonoscopy every five years after age forty if there is a family history of colon cancer or every five years after age fifty. However, patient noncompliance with these guidelines by the general U.S. population is more than 75%.

Example #2: Failure to Get Vaccinated

Hepatitis B vaccination is very effective in preventing viral Hepatitis B, which is a carcinogen for liver cancer (hepatocellular carcinoma, hepatoma). Hepatocellular carcinoma is the leading cause of cancer (750,000 per year) in the world. It accounts for 20,000 new yearly cases in the United States. The vaccine has been available to everyone in the U.S.A. for more than 20 years. The legally mandated vaccination is routinely administered to children in three injections at zero, one-month, and six-months of age. The antibody that prevents the onset of hepatitis B, produced by vaccination, is present in 92% of the U.S. population less than thirty years of age.   This percent is indicative of active immunization. However, the hepatitis B antibody for those who must voluntarily seek out vaccination, a population older than 30 years old, is less than 5%. This lack of active immunization may be due to any of the following: (1) individuals who were never immunized, or (2) the fact that the protection provided by childhood vaccinations diminishes over time without re-immunization ("booster shot"). The truth is that the need for adult immunizations never ends. Not surprisingly, approximately 50,000 adults in the United States die each year from vaccine-preventable diseases and their complications.

Example #3: Failure to Quit Smoking:

Cigarette smoking is defined as the daily use of tobacco-nicotine products continually for one to two years. Chronic cigarette use results in many of the perilous biochemical, physiological, mutagenic and carcinogenic changes that take place in otherwise normal tissues. Tissue and organ destruction that lead to major diseases that are closely linked, and now clearly appear to be caused by cigarette smoking, include the following: (1) atherosclerotic disease in non-diabetics including cerebrovascular disease, aortic aneurysm, and peripheral vascular disease, (2) chronic obstructive pulmonary disease which begins within 1-2 years after inflammatory changes begin and disappear after 1-2 years of quitting the habit, (3) cancer of the lung, larynx, oral cavity, esophagus, stomach, pancreas, kidney, urinary bladder, uterus, cervix, and breast, and (4) pregnancy complications both pre- and postnatal (e.g., miscarriage and low birth weight, respectively). Furthermore, there is an annual *associated-disease* (e.g., emphysema) death rate from chronic cigarette smoking of 400,000 individuals per year in the United States. Yet, approximately 20% of the U.S. population is still in the habit of "lighting up" on a daily basis (53% male, 47% female).

Example #4: Failure to Relieve Hypertension

Approximately 30% of American adults, aged 35 years or older, have hypertension: commonly called "high blood pressure." *Hypertension* is now defined as blood pressure in excess of 120/80. Until several years ago, it was defined as blood pressure over 140/90. The numbers, 120/80 or 140/90, are reflective of the internal pressure exerted by fluids inside the chambers of the heart as it beats to force blood through the circulatory system. Too much pressure can cause damage to cardiac (heart) muscles as well as the rupturing of blood-carrying vessels (major and minor arteries, arterioles, and capillaries). The condition is the leading primary diagnosis, in hospital inpatient and clinic outpatient settings, in the United States. It affects over 65 million individuals per year and accounts for an annual mortality of about 24,500 of our fellow citizens. Patients with hypertension die 10 to 20 years prematurely of stroke, heart disease, and kidney disease. Either preventative antihypertensive activity or alleviating antihypertensive therapy in America should be a regular part of every individual's health regimen. But, it is not. Those of us who don't "stay in shape," by eating well and exercising on a regular basis, risk developing hypertension. And, only two-thirds of hypertensive patients receive anti-hypertensive medication. Forty percent of those who do receive treatment take one drug to counter the disease, an additional 40% take two drugs, and 20% more take three drugs. Studies have shown that less than 2.5% of patients undergoing one-drug antihypertensive therapy experience a satisfactory reduction of blood pressure. Therefore, as many as 73% of hypertensive patients in the U.S. have inadequate control of their blood pressure. That's 22% of the population of American adults aged 35 years or older.

Example #5: Failure to Prevent Obesity

Fat-producing cells of the body, called *fat cells*, form *adipose tissue*. The production of too many fat cells -- that create an excess mass of adipose tissue in the organs -- has been found to cause morbidity (disease) or mortality (death). The mass of these tissues can be measured using many accurate, although often poorly available, methods. Measuring instruments have been devised to measure the thickness of skin-folds utilizing a method known as *anthropometry*. Physicians can measure underwater weight to determine a person's body density by a method called *densitometry*. And, they can measure the conductivity of bodily tissues by *electrical impedance*, taking advantage of the fact that different tissues have different resistance to weak electrical currents. However, the most widely used method to gauge body weight is the *body mass index*: or BMI. While BMI is not the most direct measure of *adiposity* (body fat) it serves to simplify the measurement terminology. As shown in FIGURE 2, titled BODY MASS INDEX, BMI is the ratio of body mass to the square of a person's height: or, mass/height^2 in kilograms per square meter (kg/m^2). The BMI of a *normal* adult is within a range of about 19 to 25 kg/m^2. A person who is considered *overweight* has a BMI of 25 to 30 kg/m^2. An *obese* person has a BMI of between 30 and 35 kg/m^2. *Morbid obesity* occurs in those having a BMI that is greater than 35 kg/m^2. An individual weighing 250 pounds at a height of 5 feet and 7 inches tall is carrying more than 80 pounds of excess weight -- due to the addition of fat cells -- than someone of equal height in the Normal Range for body weight.

FIGURE 2

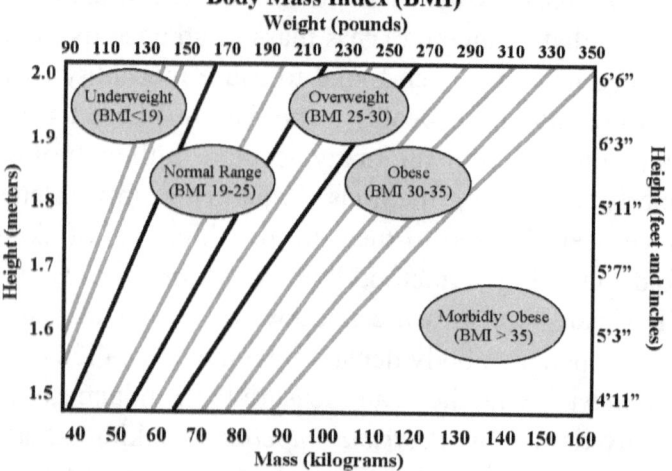

Body Mass Index (BMI)

The stress imposed on the heart and other major organs of the body is nothing less than incapacitating.

As of 2008, 59% of the U.S. adult population is fat: 30% are overweight, and 29% are obese or morbidly obese. In 1978, only 14.5% were either obese or morbidly obese. That percentage increased to 22.5% by 2001. Since then, more than an additional 6.5% of us have been paying less attention to our health than whether or not Osama bin Laden was dead or alive! Are we to rely on the fact that that murderer is finally dead to bring us back to our senses? The simple fact is that being overweight, obese, and morbidly obese is associated with many medical complications and diseases calculated to be a dozen times more common than illnesses occurring in the normal weight population. Such diseases include atherosclerotic vascular diseases, cancer, lung diseases, musculoskeletal diseases, gallstones, and diseases of the fatty organs known as *visceral steatosis*. The most significant complications of being overweight, obese, and morbidly obese are the development of hypertension, type-2 diabetes mellitus (insulin resistance) and hyperlipidemia. These latter three killers -- hypertension, diabetes mellitus, and hyperlipidemia, plus being overweight, obese, or morbidly obese -- defines *metabolic syndrome*. A diagnosis of metabolic syndrome signifies the progression of vascular disease that increases a patient's chances of having a *myocardial infarction* (heart attack) or *cerebral vascular accident* (stroke). Nowadays, weight reduction is very treatable with behavior modification, diet alteration, exercise, medication, and surgery (lap band), the treatment of choice for obese and morbidly obese individuals.

Why do so many of us keep getting fatter and fatter? And, what can we do about it?

As previously shown in FIGURE 1, two categories of chronic diseases account for 58% of yearly deaths in the United States: *atherosclerotic-related disease* and *cancer-related disease*. And, our failure to screen for cancer, get vaccinated, quit smoking, relieve hypertension, and prevent obesity is costing us hundreds of billions, if not trillions, of personal and Federal Treasury dollars.

The swift diagnosis and treatment of acute diseases that ultimately lead to chronic diseases is one of the keys to reducing Health Care costs in America. With ubiquitous and accurate monitoring and treatment of hypertension and hyperlipidemia, and by advancing weight reduction strategies in order to minimize obesity and morbid obesity, we can reduce or eliminate type-2 diabetes mellitus before the development of chronic heart, cerebral, and renal diseases occur.

By making cancer screening easy and inexpensive, a simple matter of both rational and common sense choice rather than deference to our pocket book, we can significantly deter cancer development and prolong survival by early detection with colonoscopy, Pap smear, mammogram, chest x-ray, blood and PSA tests. By so doing, these preventative medical approaches -- that treat subacute diseases such as metabolic syndrome and precancerous polyps -- can lead to the elimination of much of the cost of Health Care.

Part of the problem is that patients -- while they are feeling well -- are often complacent and unmotivated to pursue medical intervention (Preventative Health Care). Compliance is often only present when the patient is not feeling well and, after experiencing some discomfort and pain, realizes the obvious advantages of being healthy again.

What can we do to inspire patients to take an active part in their Health Care, from the point of view of prevention, in order to reduce the number of cases of subacute disease that must, in turn, lead to a reduction in the number of cases of chronic disease?

Again: Is it possible to create a Health Care system that will provide medical care for all in a fair and equitable way? While at the same time preserve freedom of choice and our individual liberties? As well as reduce the burden on citizens -- whose lifestyles already keep them healthy -- of having to pay for the lack of interest exhibited by those who fail to take care of their health?

As we see it, the task of arousing, inspiring, and motivating our fellow Americans to be more proactive in defense of their own health by complying with astutely recommended Preventative Health Care guidelines, can be accomplished in three steps.

First, it will be necessary to invest a small percentage of our tax dollars in government sponsored media programs that give the public a direct and detailed understanding of the kind of destruction that takes place in their bodies as the result of chronic disease. And, to raise awareness of the subacute diseases that inevitably lead to those chronic conditions.

This investment will yield vast returns in the form of reduced Health Care expenditures for the treatment of both subacute and chronic diseases.

The spending of tens of billions of dollars a year by pharmaceutical firms, attempting to persuade individuals who mistreat their bodies that there are medications available to "cure them," is a questionable course of action. A course of action that may lead to increases in drug company profits in the short-term but to greater expenditures in the long-term by the rest of us in the form of increased Medicare/Medicaid withholdings and rising private health insurance premiums.

It is of little value to we as a Nation for you, the reader alone, to be informed that 58% of annual deaths in the United States are related to vascular disease and cancer if that information fails to become common knowledge. It is of little value to we as a Nation for you, the reader alone, to be informed that vascular diseases such as myocardial infarction, cerebral and renal vascular, and hypertension are heralded by warning signs, symptoms, or mild illnesses -- such as metabolic syndrome -- if that information fails to sink into the public conscience. It is of no value to we as a Nation for you, the reader alone, to be informed that these relatively benign and often asymptomatic diseases -- if left untreated -- cause heart, brain, kidney, and intestinal failure if that information fails to spur every American to take action in defense of their own good health.

To put it bluntly, if people can memorize the names of their favorite professional athletes in addition to the stratospheric salaries they make -- not to mention those athlete's batting averages and yardages passed -- then they can remember specifically what happens to their heart and blood vessels when they are 20 pounds overweight and smoke.

Left untreated, invasive cancers -- such as mouth, throat, and lung cancer -- force patients into situations where aggressive and expensive surgery as well as painfully unpleasant treatments becomes a necessity. And, given the present-day state of medical care for cancer, the disease is never viewed as cured. Rather, it is viewed as "being in remission:" an ongoing condition that is medically approached as a chronic disease, a condition that places the patient into the situation of being a "cancer survivor." Thereby, affecting all aspects of life, and often making their quality of life unacceptable to the patient with increased emotions of fear, depression, and grieving.

Think how relatively easy it is to undergo laboratory urine, blood and other body fluid tests, imaging tests, including ultrasound, CT scan, MRI, PET scan, endoscopy and colonoscopy. Compare those patient experiences of having to endure the discomfort of invasive diagnostic tests and the horror of living with heart disease, renal disease, cerebral vascular disease, and the almost unendurable hospital stays coincident with the throbbing pain of angioplasty, stent placement, arterial bypass and transplant surgeries of heart, liver, and kidneys.

Chronic vascular diseases and cancer are devastating to patients, their families and friends, because of the life-changing events that must follow.

The wide and continual dissemination of preventative medical approaches that inform and educate our citizens is not only fiscally sound and sensible but ethically desirable if not morally compulsory. Especially in light of the fact that -- with present day medication, computerized technology, and continuing research -- these potentially fierce and devastating disorders can be brought under control: thereby, enhancing our quality and longevity of life.

Our failure as a nation to assure that every citizen is informed -- and repeatedly reminded -- of the absolute necessity to undergo regular health screening as recommended under Preventative Health Care guidelines has resulted in the unnecessary expenditure of hundreds of billions of dollars that would otherwise remain in the hands of its citizens: to be spent according to their own needs and desires.

Our politicians -- on both sides of the aisle -- give a lot of lip service to "stimulating the economy." Well, you have just read part of the solution to that dilemma explaining in good part how to do it.

In the field of Preventative Health Care, patient motivation and compliance, proactivity and persistence are essential. Therefore, the problem compounding Health Care costs -- that is hardly ever addressed in any Health Care discussion -- is convincing and then placing the patient into a proactive Health Care delivery model.

Patient proactivity can only become routine through self-motivation, will power, and a positive attitude. However, in order to arrive at that point, the critical and extensive education of patients -- almost to the point of understanding end-organ failure and the final results of end-stage diseases -- becomes imperative. Re-educating our citizenry to become more attentive to their quality of life, and to have an optimistic outlook, is essential.

The next step in the task of arousing, inspiring, and motivating our fellow Americans to be more proactive in defense of their own health is no less important than the first.

Secondly, it is important that every American feels confident that there are few real obstacles standing between them and their good health: not the government, nor their insurance company, nor their pocket book.

A lot has been written concerning the psychology of physically feeling good. If you think you feel good, you physically feel good, and vice versa. And, this relationship is not just "touchy-feely" rhetoric. There are direct physiological and biochemical relationships between having a realistically confident, positive attitude and one's physical and mental well-being.

Biochemicals, called *metabolic mediators*, that control cellular, tissue, and organ functions throughout the body and brain are activated by anger, tension, anxiety, depression, and overall emotional distress. These hormones, biochemical messengers, and neurotransmitters -- such as cortisol, epinephrine (adrenaline), norepinephrine, and acetylcholine -- stimulate a variety of regions in the central nervous system (CNS) and *pituitary-adrenal axis*.

The pituitary-adrenal axis is one of the major metabolic systems that coordinate action between the brain and body through the action of glands. Under any number of circumstances, these systems are activated to cause vasoconstriction, elevated blood pressure, decreased arterial-venous blood flow, and platelet stickiness that determines how well and fast our blood will clot. Improper clot formation, alone, can lead to cardiac and cerebral arterial occlusion that can cause a heart attack or stroke. And, it is essential to note, that feeling lousy -- because the government can't make up their mind about how to solve the Health Care Crisis, or that your insurance company refuses to pay for a diagnostic exam or the therapy that can alleviate your pain, or that your premiums and copayments have become so exorbitant that you have to go without eating for several days to afford them -- will set off a blast in a host of biochemical systems that can adversely affect your health. There is a biological "pathophysiological" relationship between *emotionally* feeling good versus bad and *physically* feeling good versus bad.

Feeling good plays an important role in protecting us against diseases that ravage our cardio-cerebral vascular system or augment the development of cancer. Pursuing a course of Preventative Health Care can significantly reduce the average person's stress, anxiety, and depression. While the same positive course of action can decrease the likelihood of developing diseases like hypertension and diabetes mellitus as well as cancer. At the same time, nurturing a life style that promotes the proper functioning of our cells, tissues, and organs helps to minimize the chances of developing a disease that can impact our psychological well-being. Feeling good promotes healthier bodily functions. While healthy bodily functions increases our chances of feeling good. It's not so much "mind over matter" versus "matter over mind" as it is "body and soul" working in tandem: each dependent on the other to manifest good health.

It is imperative -- during this time of wondrous medical knowledge and technology -- that both physicians and patients, together, grasp the opportunity for the advancement of our *mental and physical well-being*. Rather than expecting our doctors to "save us" we must seek knowledge rather than be complacent. And, we must use that knowledge to fend off illness. Achieving this healthful metamorphosis is sure to lead us to follow a straight and narrow path through life no matter how many times we are tempted by unhealthy detours. The core concept of this entire transformation is *optimism*. With regards to good health, optimism is as essential a component of our psychology as a balanced diet is to our physiology.

The final step in the task of arousing, inspiring, and motivating our fellow Americans to be more proactive in defense of their own health is perhaps the most important of the three.

Last but not least, it will become necessary to provide every American with a *fair and equitable financial incentive* that accrues monetary benefits to those proactive individuals who make the maintenance of their personal health a matter of routine. For the most part, as Americans, we favor *giving* charity over *receiving* it. But, we instinctively shun those who choose to take advantage of us rather than making their best effort to provide for themselves and their families. Since the days of Washington and Jefferson, it has been a part of our national conscience to take responsibility for defending the freedoms our *Constitution* enshrines. And as such, we expect our neighbors to feel and act the same way. We rely upon them to favor us with fair and equitable treatment, especially in matters of trade. It is time we rewarded those proactively healthy individuals who have been paying into government and private health insurance programs without receiving a financial return on their investment.

In a truly fair and free market economy, both producer and consumer stand to gain from a fair and evenhanded exchange. We value the "win-win scenario." So, if we as a nation of taxpayers are all to contribute a percentage of our hard-earned income to make sure that every individual has access to excellent and affordable Health Care, it is only fair and equitable that those individuals who behave proactively in defense of our own good health -- and therefore put less burden on the Treasury -- benefit financially from their actions. With enough money in the Treasury to pay for the Health Care needs of all Americans -- a feat that can be accomplished under the plan proposed in *Chapter 7* -- we will be able afford to "hold out a carrot" to those who currently lack the will to do as they must do. There is no better enticement than a tempting monetary incentive.

Tax rebate, anyone?

All you have to do is listen to your competent and compassionate physician and muster the will power to do what he/she recommends!

To reiterate the challenge: Is it possible -- in a nation that has thrived on a fair and free market economy -- to create a cost-effective, efficient, and compassionate Health Care system that manages to *stay in the black* without restricting individual liberties. No matter how foolhardy the "liberties" taken by the risk takers among us happen to be?

We confidently conclude that it is. If and only if, we place the sole responsibility for seeking out competent medical care providers on the individual customer who requires their services: the patient.

In a truly fair and free market economy, the solution to our Nation's Health Care problems rests on the sound relationship between *both a competent physician and a cooperative patient*. As a team, there is no challenge they cannot face and overcome together with "good old-fashioned American drive and know-how" and tried and true American conviction and daring.

Given that, the only obstacle that would remain in our endeavor to reduce Health Care costs is the necessity to neutralize obstructing barriers -- created by nonessential "middle men" currently working in the system -- that create roadblocks to bar our way.

Chapter 5

A Brief History of Health Care and
How We Got Into This Mess

****

Abstract

Despite great advances in the medical sciences and the accumulation of statistical, evidenced-based studies of medications and treatments, it is still crucial to the sensible practice of medicine that doctors know their patients well. Yet, Health Care in America has evolved from a "horizontally integrated price elastic fee-for-service" industry -- comprised of independent physician-providers and patient-customers once totally in command of decisions regarding medical care -- to a "vertically integrated price inelastic service" -- comprised of top-down managed, government and insurance industry middle-men who interfere with the medical decisions made by doctors and their patients. Whereas the contributions made by insurance companies were "a good idea at the time" they entered the market during the Industrial Revolution of the 19th Century, they have become an obsolete hindrance to the efficient functioning of a fair and free market medical care industry. Fundamentally, the solution to the Health Care Crisis facing America, today, involves the establishment of a unique new system of Health Care. This system must permit the fair and free market to dominate, allowing highly competent and compassionate physicians and their patients to make all decisions regarding medical care. It must reward citizens who do their best to stay healthy, and give all Americans in time of need the freedom to choose the best providers the industry has to offer.

****

Two weeks before the Christmas holidays in December of 1799, Dr. James Craik -- a prominent Virginian physician -- was called to care for a longtime friend who was suffering from laryngitis and pneumonia. It seemed his patient had spent nearly all the previous day inspecting his farm land, riding on horseback through snow which by mid-afternoon had become freezing hail and chilling rain. That evening, the landowner -- also of some notoriety -- came home to dinner and, famished, ate without changing his soaking wet clothing. The following morning, he awoke coughing, sneezing and feverish. The patient complained that he was having trouble breathing and was finding it difficult to swallow. Noting the seriousness of the condition, Dr. Craik summoned two other physicians to assist him: Drs. Elisha C. Dick and Gustavus Richard Brown. In their efforts to aid their patient, the three doctors employed the standard treatments of the day: bloodletting, the application of poultices, and a rectal solution of calomel and tartar. The bloodletting of thirty-two ounces of blood, it was thought, would remove toxins from their patient's body that had thrown his "humors" out of balance. The poultices -- warm, soft and moist, cloth wrappings of flour and other plant material -- were applied to the patient's neck and chest to relieve inflammation and soreness. To clean the patient's lower intestines, enemas of calomel and tartar -- solutions of mercury chloride and potassium bitartate -- were performed to initiate a copious release of the bowels. In addition, the ill man inhaled warm vapors of vinegar and water and ingested ten grains of calomel followed by repeated doses of tartar to make him vomit.

The patient's condition continued to deteriorate.

Dr. Dick suggested that a tracheotomy be performed to relieve the patient's breathing difficulty. However, Drs. Craik and Brown decided against Dick's suggestion, since the danger of infection resulting from the risky operative procedure was more likely to worsen the condition. In more antiseptic modern times, of course, the procedure could have been lifesaving. Drs. Craik and Brown made their best judgment given the methodology of their time. Dr. Dick would later write the following unfavorable opinion of the two physicians:

> "I know not what might have been the result and it would be presumption to pronounce upon it; but I shall never cease to regret that the operation was not performed."

Several months later, in polite deference to Dr. Dick, Dr. Brown wrote the following to Dr. Cralk:

> "Sir: I have lately met Dr. Dick again in consultation and the high opinion that I formed of him when we were in conference last month, concerning the situation of our illustrious friend, has been confirmed. You remember how, by his clear reasoning and evident knowledge of the cause of certain symptoms after the examination of the General, he assured us that it was not really quinsy, which we supposed it

to be, but a violent inflammation of the membranes of the throat, which it had almost closed, and which if not immediately arrested would result in his death. You must remember he was averse to bleeding the General, and I have often thought that if we had acted accordingly to his suggestion, when he said, 'he needs all his strength - bleeding will diminish it,' and taken no more blood from him, our good friend might have been alive now. But we were governed by the best light we had: we thought we were right, and so we were justified."

Their patient's condition worsened all the next day, and at 10 pm on the evening of December 14, 1799, the First President of the United States of America, General George Washington, died of complications from a simple sore throat, then called a Quincy sore throat, that progressed to an infectious peritonsilar abscess.

Washington's last words were "'Tis well."

From the scientific perspective, "governed by the best light" they had, the practices of physicians Craik, Brown, and Dick did not change for more than a century. Until, advances in physics, chemistry, and biology gave doctors new theories and technology with which to better diagnose and treat illness.

As mentioned previously, the research and discoveries of Louis Pasteur in the mid-19th Century, revolutionized the medical community's conception of the origin of diseases and their causes due to microorganisms. Pasteur, with the chemist Claude Bernard, developed *pasteurization*: the process that removes harmful bacteria from milk and other animal products. Together, their experiments added strength to their revolutionary germ theory. Pasteur, along with the biologist Robert Koch, founded bacteriology. Koch became renowned for his discovery of the tubercle bacillus in 1882 and the cholera bacillus in 1883. Medical students know him best for his development of *Koch's postulates*: a set of guidelines for culturing and isolating bacteria for experimental purposes. And, while many conservative physicians unable to see the scientific value of these new approaches delayed advancement in the medical arts, more open-minded physicians like the British surgeon Joseph Lister adopted the practices of these experimental scientists. Lister is known for developing the *principles of antisepsi*s in the treatment of infectious wounds. Today, a popular treatment for halitosis is named after him. Ever hear of *Listerine®*?

With the publication of *The Origin of Species by Means of Natural Selection* by Charles Darwin's in 1859, a revolution in biology and medicine led to an equally tumultuous revolution in chemistry that gains steam to this very day. In addition, the lost work of Gregor Mendel -- who first published his work on the heredity of pea plants in 1865 -- was rediscovered at the turn of the 20th century. *Mendel's Laws* became the foundation of *classical genetics*: a body of work that -- within five short decades -- led to the discovery of the structure of DNA in 1953 by James Watson, Francis Crick, and Rosalind Franklin. Their work is the foundation of molecular biology and modern genetics.

The last 150 years has been an era in which the scientific method as been employed to find cures for a wide range of endemic infectious diseases. With the advancement of physics and the materials sciences, chemical, electrical, and mechanical engineers have rushed to invent a profusion of valuable diagnostic and treatment technologies.

World War I saw the first use of x-ray technology and the electrocardiograph for monitoring internal bodily functions. In addition to these inventions, medical scientists of the time developed new anti-bacterial agents: such as the sulfonamide (sulfa) antibiotics. World War II saw the development of penicillin antibiotics, produced by British and American pharmaceutical scientists. The widespread use of these new chemicals in antimicrobial therapy has since saved billions of lives throughout the world.

Rapid availability in these medical technologies has not only changed the way doctors diagnose and treat disease it has changed the way they view their patients -- for better and worse -- resulting in the widely used practice of *evidence-based medicine*.

In the last half-century, analysts have performed thousands of statistical studies designed to measure the effectiveness of medical products and treatment strategies. The analyses of different populations of individuals affected by hundreds of different diseases and afflictions have yielded valuable data: information that a new generation of physicians can consider in their diagnosis and treatment of illness. These studies comprise the basis for evidence-based medicine (EBM) or evidence-based practice (EBP).

To this day, the gathering and statistical analysis of information from a multitude of clinical trials and hospital studies is intended to assist physicians in clinical-decision-making by providing them with the best available evidence gleaned from the scientific method. This evidence is intended to help doctors to assess the risks and benefits of treatments and diagnostic tests or -- for that matter -- the *withholding* of treatment and diagnostic tests. These studies frequently include the systematic reviews of controlled clinical trials (double-blind or placebo-controlled studies) and the analysis of the conventional wisdom of many thousands of long-practicing physicians.

Yet, while most physicians have come to increasingly rely on EBM/EBP, there are many who find it just as valuable to simply *know and look at their patient*. These physicians recognize that knowledge of individual factors -- such as a patient's quality-of-life value judgments -- must go hand-in-hand with reference to evidence-based analysis and practice. They realize that a patient's personal behavior -- factors frequently more difficult to analyze using the scientific method -- are as relevant to their development of proper diagnosis and treatment recommendations as data gleaned from clinical trials. These doctors accept the fact that scientific studies and statistics (risk-benefit analysis, randomized trials, and the review of medical literature) have value *only after a direct and thorough patient examination by a competent physician.*

It is disturbing to note that -- in the vast majority of cases today -- patients admitted to hospitals rarely see the physician responsible for their care. Instead, patients are tended by nurses and nursing assistants who pass on information regarding a patient's condition to a doctor sitting in front of a computer console, sifting through data that is immediately correlated with statistically evaluated evidence-based therapeutic recommendations. Only after the physician makes their decision regarding their "assigned patient" do they visit that patient to notify them of the decided upon course of treatment. All too frequently, too many doctors are starting to treat patients as statistics rather than individual human beings.

In point of fact, statisticians consistently remind us that statistical studies say nothing about the individual participants taking part in their studies. Statistics is the practice of collecting and analyzing numerical data from large populations of individuals for the purpose of inferring proportions emerging from those populations ("Half the population improved with the use of the drug."). Scores that rate particular behaviors or characteristics of single individuals become nothing more than minute pieces of data, among thousands of pieces of data, put through the mathematical meat grinder to identify *population trends*: not individual uniqueness.

For example: A teacher's statistical analysis of math test results might show that the average test score was 50%. However, that statistic does not mean that everyone who took the test is a moron and that every student must be re-taught the concepts assessed by the test. Drawing such a conclusion from that statistical result, and taking such subsequent action based on that result, would be erroneous: not merely a waste of time but counterproductive for those students who scored well on the test and who are prepared to move one to the next phase of learning. Likewise, a pharmaceutical company's statistical study of a drug's effects might show that 70% of the patients exhibiting particular disease symptoms "benefited" by administration of their new drug. However, that statistic does not mean that every patient will benefit from its use. In fact, the drug might seriously harm many individuals using it. We have all read the warnings on drug labels and heard drug company television commercials disclosing the "side effects" of their products.

Before prescribing any treatment or medication, a competent physician *must know their patient* and consider the risks of such a treatment against its benefits. The risk vs. benefit data -- made available through EBM -- of any diagnostic technology or treatment may prove helpful. But, unfortunately, it has become more common for physicians to rely increasingly on that data rather than closely considering the medical history of their patients. Especially in the emergency room and/or hospital setting where doctors are meeting patients for the first time. Here broadens the "risk *vs.* benefit analysis dilemma" faced -- every day -- by every physician regarding the direct medical care of every patient.

A patient suffering from autoimmune hepatitis -- a liver disease that causes the concentration of ammonia to rise in the blood resulting in a state of mental confusion called "foggy brain" -- does not necessarily need a referral to a neurologist. Such a referral would not be unusual for a physician working in today's vertically integrated Health Care system, attempting to diagnose a new patient; since, it is an evidenced-based referral to which many physicians would be drawn upon hearing the complaint of a patient that they were experiencing "mental confusion." Un-familiar with the complete ramifications of a patient's individual condition, might easily lead the referred neurologist to order a series of invasive and expensive neurological tests! Given that a good percentage of the "mentally confused" individuals encountered by that neurologist had brain tumors. In this case, as in so many others, the phrase "Better safe than sorry" might as easily be read "Better that I don't get sued in the event the patient actually has a brain tumor."

To reiterate, it takes *a competent physician who knows their patient and their medical history* -- not merely a statistical analysis -- to make decisions as to whether or not that unique patient needs a particular diagnostic assessment or therapy. For many of us, the impersonal nature of statistical analysis has given rise to the feeling that we are "just another statistic."

Sadly, physicians are more increasingly required to base their medical decisions for individual patients directly on evidence-based statistical analysis. Much of this requirement stems directly from the reality that physicians -- and their malpractice insurance attorneys -- need "evidence" to present in court on their client's behalf in the event of a lawsuit. Doctors are being compelled to base their diagnoses and treatments more on evidence-based studies than direct examination and patient health history. The result is the ordering of unnecessary tests and treatments that increases the cost of Health Care in America without enhancing the well-being of patients. It has come to pass that *ex cathedra* (authoritative) statements made by "medical experts (physicians)" are considered less valid than the statistical analysis of whole populations. Long-term statistical studies that cost the American taxpayer many tens of millions of dollars per study!

More and more physicians are beginning to reassess the actual value of EBM and EBP. They understand that medical research analysis and the use of available diagnostic and treatment technology -- for the simple reason that it is readily available -- have their limitations. Research data and technology are merely tools to be utilized by astute and caring physicians familiar with their patients' medical case histories: a practice we've moved away from in this country. Regardless of where a physician has been trained, the delivery of Health Care has become, almost exclusively, technology and EBM/EBP driven. Rather than first looking at the patient and their medical history, a physician's evaluation is too often based solely on the technology of multiple imaging studies and laboratory tests, and potentially flawed pharmacological research funded by a pharmaceutical industry that profits from the sale of many questionable medications.

The physician's clinical hands-on diagnoses of their patient, and the physician's knowledge and analytical ability (their *ex cathedra* judgments), have become marginalized. There is often negligible attention to differential diagnosis (the determination of which one of several diseases may be producing symptoms), and an increasing tendency among medical specialists (cardiologists, oncologists, neurologists, rheumatologists, etc.) to diagnose patients as having an ailment in their own area of medical expertise. More upsetting is the trend to lose a sense of compassionate concern and caring for the patient in the translation from evidence-based data to direct patient care and treatment.

The time has come for a reassessment of the risk *vs.* benefits analysis of diagnostic tests and treatments and for a reaffirmation of the primary importance of the *physician-patient relationship* over the *statistician-patient relationship* in the practice of medicine.

As such, there has been a growing movement toward the evaluation of the effectiveness of drugs and other treatments already in widespread use. Called *comparative effectiveness research* (CER), these studies are designed to determine which kinds of existing treatments work and which do not.

Given the enormous advances of computer and internet technology, hospitals and physicians groups have allied in a effort to "mine the data base" containing accessible information on patients suffering from a variety of specific medical conditions. Respecting the confidentiality of individual patient information, analyses are conducted in order to discover which drugs and treatments are already working on individuals sharing the same medical conditions and histories (specific symptoms and diagnoses, severity of disorder, age, personal habits, etc.): information supplied by *physicians who know their patients*. The approach has some definite advantages over costly clinical trials (studies used to evaluate the effectiveness of new drugs and therapies) that often analyze randomly selected populations of individuals who happen to be showing symptoms common to a particular illness. Frequently, these studies rely on otherwise healthy young individuals who are paid to participate in the study. Instead, CER has the advantage of mining the existing data bank to focus on evaluating the effectiveness of specific therapies already used in specific cases.

At a time when the costs of Health Care are on the rise, it is imperative that we avail ourselves of the information on hand to discover those specifically effective treatments already in the medical armory. Without efforts like CER, the accelerating overuse of the medical advancements of the last half-century, having impacted all aspects of diagnosis and treatment, will continue to contribute to the ever-increasing cost of doing medicine: a cost inflated by the profiteering of those who benefit monetarily *from the overuse* of medications and technologies used by physicians.

We have all seen commercial advertisements directed at the general public, costing billions of dollars to put on the air, by drug companies attempting to persuade customers to ask their physicians about new drugs on the market. Drugs that have been evaluated for effectiveness in clinical-trial studies paid for by those same companies. Patients have effectively been drafted into the sales force of billion-dollar pharmaceutical firms.

Of course, those innovative and inventive individuals who develop new medicines and medical technology, put to good use by the medical community, are certainly entitled to benefit financially for their contributions. While the rapidly expanding costs of Health Care is to some extent the result of their aggressive marketing strategies, there are few who would deny them their profits for having made life healthier for many of us. However, freeing doctors to focus more on the personal relationship between themselves and their patient, so that they might better recommend only those tests and treatments that are absolutely necessary given their knowledge of their patient, is sure to reduce Health Care costs. Wasting time listening to drug company salespeople, bombarding them with free samples to disseminate among their patients, increases the inefficiency of any physician's practice.

In addition, there are other more excessive expenditures plaguing the medical field that continue to accelerate the rising price of Health Care. Money that is siphoned from those who provide direct medical services (hospitals, doctors, nurses, medical technicians, etc.) into the hands of those who profit without contributing to the well-being of a single patient. There are those who do nothing to aid the infirm but, instead, frequently impede the efforts of those fighting to return to good health. As mentioned in the *Chapter 1*, the simple fact is that, in present day America, there are too many players in the game: profit-seeking, corporate players that drive up medical costs -- unnecessarily -- without ever lifting a finger to improve the health of a single patient or lessen the burdens of the physicians who treat them.

Both physicians and patients are asking the question: "Who is in charge of our health care?"

They are beginning to observe that enormous health care entities have essentially replaced the individual physician when it comes to how, where, when, and even why medical care is dispensed. This growth in the number of Health Care players has led to a major disconnect between the individual and the medical personnel dispensing care. As in other sectors of our economy, profiteers who "offer their services" to those who actually provide a service to customers have invaded the medical care industry, thus raising the cost of those services to consumers.

Ironically, despite the successes of the fair and free market economy that built this great Nation, and despite the warnings of President George Washington in his *Farewell Address* to the Nation on September 19, 1796, the forces of greed and undue political party influences remain hard at work shackling the most innovative entrepreneurs among us in all sectors of our economy. This has been done, and continues to be done, by those whose affluence has empowered them to skew the economy in favor of themselves for the purpose of protecting their own personal wealth at the expense of *genuine free enterprise*.

In the case of Health Care, it all began with a perfectly fair and reasonable free market innovation.

Throughout the 19th Century, the expansion of American industry (railroads, river commerce, steel, textiles, agriculture, mining, etc.) was accompanied by an increase in job related accidents and health problems. The new technologies were -- by virtue of being new -- frequently unperfected and unsafe, resulting in injuries at the mills and disease at the mines (black lung). Injury and death proliferated across production lines. Since the loss of a well-trained and experienced worker, for days or weeks on end, was (and still is) of concern to employers, a means of "insuring" the ongoing health of the work force was sought.

At a time when the practice of medicine was performed on a "fee for service" business model, a small group of businessmen saw a solution to the problem. Motivated to make a profit based on sound actuarial analysis to cover their potential losses, they offered workers the opportunity to "protect their earnings" in the event of personal disaster and to assure their return to work as soon as possible. Actuarial analysis helped "insurers" to compile statistics and calculate their company's monetary risk of increased expenses (payouts to injured clients) against the collection of steady income-producing premiums from customers (cash income).

New *insurance companies* were set up to provide a needed service to both workers and their employers while at the same time making a reasonable profit for insurance firms. Insurance firms accomplish this by actuarially "hedging their bets," across a client population of both healthy and potentially ill individuals, in much the same way that any horse racing bookie assures himself a profit by "laying off wagers" on a number of differentially skilled equine contestants. The only difference between the two service industries -- insurance vs. gambling -- is that in the horse racing game the gambler loses if his horse loses the race. In the health insurance industry, on the other hand, the premium-paying client "loses" a heck of a lot of money if he stays healthy over the course of his lifetime before suddenly dying of a stroke. Still, while that premium-paying client paid out hundreds of thousands (perhaps millions) of dollars in premiums, he "profited" by knowing that he and his family would not become destitute as the result of some serious accident or long-term chronic illness. At the same time, the insurance company profited by their customers staying healthy and could only be put out of business by some contagious disease or epidemic of accidents. It seemed an equitable arrangement, and was -- at one time -- a win-win scenario.

The *Franklin Health Assurance Company of Massachusetts*, a firm founded in 1850, offered insurance against injuries arising from railroad and steamboat accidents. By the mid-1860s, there were sixty organizations offering accident insurance in the United States, an industry that consolidated -- as did many other industries (railroads, river commerce, steel, textiles, agriculture, mining, etc.) -- soon thereafter.

Enter trusts and monopolies.

Following the Civil War, and for decades to come, American industry expanded by leaps and bounds. The most successful industries -- such as the railroad and steel industries -- took the lead by consolidating their interests, profiting all the more by "squeezing" competitors out of their markets. This was often accomplished by getting their own industry leaders and legal associates elected or appointed to government office at both the state and federal levels. As government officials, these politicians could further the wealthy aspirations of their industrial benefactors by passing laws that favored their control over more and more sectors of the economy.

We were forewarned of these "factions and cabals" for personal gain by President Washington in his *Farewell Address*. In that address, the First President presaged the disastrous consequences resulting from the actions that such selfish consortiums would have on a fair and free trade economy.

As the 20th Century approached, industry magnates continued to seek ways to evade even the weakest existing laws restricting their attempts to unfairly favor their own companies. In one such case in 1879, attorneys for the *Standard Oil Company of Ohio* created a trust agreement that did an "end run" around legal prohibitions of the time that made it illegal for corporations to own stock in other corporations. A trust is a contract that permits one party to "entrust" their property to a second party: property that can then be used under specified conditions for profitable gain by that second party. This tactic allowed Standard Oil to gain controlling interests in the companies of its competitors for the purpose of eliminating fair market competition.

Of course, fair and free market competition is the force that drives down the cost of products and services as business owners do their darnedest to attract customers by lowering prices. *Standard Oil* became a monopoly. A *monopoly* is a group of companies that takes exclusive possession of, and exercises exclusive control over, the supply or trade of some commodity or service. *Standard Oil's* monopoly on products and services allowed them to control (read "raise") prices on those products and services. It gave them the power to charge whatever they liked to pad their earnings and increase their holdings and political influence. Such a tactic would have made Adam Smith, the "father of American capitalism," sick to his stomach. The Founding Fathers must have been -- and in light of most recent events surely still are -- turning in their graves.

The United States Congress of the late 19th Century sensed a cloud over the free market and, in 1890, passed the *Sherman Act (The Sherman Antitrust Act)*: named after its author, Senator John Sherman. After being ratified by the Senate and passed unanimously by the House of Representatives on June 20, 1890, the *Act* was signed into law on July 2 by President Benjamin Harrison.

The *Sherman Act* gave the federal government the power to investigate and dismember trusts, companies, and other business organizations suspected of violating its provisions. The law was specifically written to prevent industrial conglomerates from artificially raising prices by restricting trade or controlling the supply and distribution of goods and services. An "innocent" monopoly, run by businessmen of merit, who earned their wealth by providing customers with better and cheaper products and services, was (and still is) perfectly legal. But, "conspiring" monopolists who serve their own ends for the purpose of preserving their own wealthy status are not.

The Sherman Act was not written to protect competitors. It was written to protect competition.

Nevertheless, for the next decade elected and appointed politicians serving the nefarious interests of wealthy corporate monopolies were unwilling to use the new law in defense of a fair and free market. Despite a few legal actions taken under the law, the most illustrious taken against the *American Railway Union* to settle a strike by Pullman railroad car workers, the act was not invoked in earnest until President Theodore Roosevelt took office in 1901. Roosevelt used the *Sherman Act* to break up the *Northern Securities Company*: a securities monopoly formed in 1902 by the wealthy corporate magnates J. P. Morgan, J. D. Rockefeller, and their associates for the purpose of controlling more than a dozen railroad companies. The United States Government sued the monopoly that same year under the provisions of the *Sherman Act*. Roosevelt's successor, President William Howard Taft later used the Act to splinter the American Tobacco Company.

Despite some early successes achieved under the enforcement provisions of the *Sherman Act*, greedy corporate executives still try to unfairly "hedge their bets" by hampering free market competition by "hook or crook." These efforts are frequently assisted by many of our less than ethical politicians. What is more astonishingly true is the fact that monopolies formed by insurance companies in particular -- among them the health insurance arm of their service industry -- are not subject to the investigative and enforcement provisions of the *Sherman Act*!

Legislation and Supreme Court rulings of the past (and present) continue to favor that industry. Insurance firms are -- to this day -- immune to much federal regulation and law enforcement provisions under the *Sherman Act*. This incredible state of affairs has been made possible, in part, by the fact that government authorities have been duped -- thus far -- into accepting the preposterous notion that insurance companies are not subject to investigation, regulation, or prosecution by the Federal government; because, the sale of insurance services are interpreted -- under present laws -- *as not qualifying as interstate commerce*. Instead, insurance companies are merely subject to limited and weak regulations placed into law by individual States, whose politicians frequently come to power with the help of campaign contributions made by those same insurance companies.

The *McCarran-Ferguson Act*, passed by Congress in 1945, is a federal law that excludes the insurance business from much federal regulation, including many federal anti-trust and monopoly laws enacted under the *Sherman Act*. Congress passed the law following a ruling by the Supreme Court in the case of the *United States v. South-Eastern Underwriters Association*. The high court had ruled in that case that the Federal Government could only regulate insurance companies under the authority of the *Commerce Clause* of the *U.S. Constitution*, which bars the Fed from usurping the regulatory responsibilities of individual States.

The *Commerce Clause*, under Article II, Section 8.3 of the *Constitution* enumerating the *General Powers of Congress*, states that Congress shall have the power ...

> "To regulate Commerce with foreign Nations, and among the several States, and with the Indian Tribes."

The phrase "*among* the several states" [italics ours] implies that Congress does not have the power to regulate commerce within a given State, while giving it explicit power to regulate dealings between business entities doing business across state lines. However, the Supreme Court's ruling in the case of the *United States v. South-Eastern Underwriters Association* interpreted the *Commerce Clause* to mean that Congress had the power to *decide* whether to regulate interstate commerce, or not to regulate it, given particular circumstances. The ruling -- in effect -- left the choice "to regulate or not to regulate" interstate commerce, specifically in the matter of the insurance industry, up to Congress. Of course, our elected representatives sitting in the United States Congress also frequently come to power with the help of campaign contributions made by insurance companies. Following the Supreme Court's ruling in the case of the *United States v. South-Eastern Underwriters Association*, the authors of the *McCarran–Ferguson Act* stipulated that Federal anti-trust laws do not apply to the insurance business as long as a given State already regulates some of that business *within* its own State. No matter how widespread the insurance business is in its operations across state lines.

That's like insisting that Congress be forbidden from regulating the dealings of truck companies delivering fertilizer across state lines, because the States bordering those state lines already limit how fast truck company drivers can drive in their State. If they were protected by such legal subterfuge, truck companies -- like insurance companies already immune to Federal laws like the Sherman Act -- could ban together to form monopolies and arbitrarily raise prices for their deliveries.

Despite the absurd reasoning of the authors of the *McCarran-Ferguson Act*, the *Commerce Clause* still empowers Congress to regulate the commerce of businesses that do business "among the several States" regardless of the State laws already in place to regulate that business. In effect, the *McCarran-Ferguson Act* attempts to prevent the Federal Government from superseding the laws of individual states, which must happen when its obligation to *"promote the general Welfare"* -- as stipulated in the *Preamble to the Constitution* -- is at stake. As in the case of a State denying a block of citizens the right to vote because they are a minority race.

Today, the health insurance industry remains under the protection of the *McCarran-Ferguson Act*, making it legal for them to control pricing and industry aligned contractual practices regarding the distribution of services across their industry and across the country, regardless of the number of "competitors" they claim provide those services.

As captive customers of the health insurance industry, we are so accustomed to having them "serve us," that many of us find it disconcerting that there are more than 40,000,000 Americans who remain "uninsured." Few stop to think that the health insurance industry -- since its inception -- has never eased the pain of a single patient. Yet, our legislators continue to try to find ways to "tweak" health insurance plans and contracts presumably for the purpose of "improving Health Care." That strategy is tantamount to adding more cinnamon and sugar to a recipe for pumpkin pie containing cow manure as its prime ingredient! And we wonder why our concern over the state of Health Care in our country leaves a lousy taste in our mouths.

The reality is that we don't need to provide our citizens with more health insurance! We need to provide them with better and less expensive medical care!

For decades, insurance providers have been acting as superfluous middlemen who profit by processing financial transactions between doctors and patients *after* they -- the insurers -- decide whether or not *they* -- the insurers -- want to pay those bills out of their premium assets. As we all know, insurance company accountants -- some posing as non-practicing physicians making judgments regarding medical treatments -- now have rights under contract law to decide which medical products and services doctors and patients are permitted to use!

The news is filled with stories of lawsuits filed by individuals (and groups) whose health coverage has been denied, and of insurers blatantly ignoring the terms of their contractual agreements with patients. Few injured plaintiffs are awarded damages while most never bother to file complaints for fear that monies spent on legal services will run out before they can recover for damages. Hospitals spend hundreds of millions of dollars processing claims that are fought by insurers who ultimately deny those claims, and many go bankrupt for failing to collect monies owed them by insurance companies. As an added expense to the cost of doing medicine, individual doctors and physicians groups must hire additional bookkeeping personnel to do the same. Under the *McCarran-Ferguson Act*, all these "profit-padding" insurance company practices are legal!

Today, there are eight major health insurers whose profits remain virtually identical, year-after-year, despite their fervent claims that they are arduously competing against one another to bring down the cost of Health Care: *Aetna, Blue Cross Blue Shield Association, CIGNA, Kaiser Permanente, Humana, Health Net, United Health Group, and Wellpoint.* Together, the overlapping investments of these giant corporations hold controlling interest in hundreds of smaller companies, making the term "competition," a laughable window-dressing front. Picture the character Don Corleone in the movie *Godfather* smoking a cigar in the office of his "olive oil importing" company. The blood on the floor is hardly visible through the smoke.

From the late 1960's into the early 1970's, along with rapid advances in medical technology in all aspects of diagnosis, medical, and surgical treatment -- that made the cost of medical care more and more expensive -- came three transformations that took place almost simultaneously in the medical field: transformations that have made the cost of Health Care even more expensive.

First, the practice of medicine changed from being a *horizontally integrated "fee-for-service"* Health Care system to a *vertically integrated "managed care system"* divided into three insurance subgroups: health management organizations (HMO's), hospital-based organizations such as Kaiser (HBO's), and private physician organizations (PPO's).

Second, as a result of that transition, doctors were lured -- out of economic necessity -- to become contractually obligated to a host of private insurance companies and begin treating patients as captive subjects: patients unable to choose their doctor from among a host of independent medical service providers and networks. Since then, patients have no longer had the right to freely choose their own doctor or hospital from a pool of fairly competitive medical providers. If we do "go out of network" we pay heavily for our "disloyalty."

Third, a new generation of physicians, both foreign and domestic, from the day they graduated from medical school (with D's or better), were systematically guaranteed an influx of customers under contract with HMO's, HBO's, and PPO's. Of this new generation, there were many who have set aside their *Hippocratic Oath* -- assuming they ever swore to it -- for benefit of financial gain and wealth at the expense patient care.

Together, these three transformations, designed to "insure" the health of the general public, became a drag on the *fair and free market practice of finding the best doctor*. By disallowing the individual customer the chance to seek out the best and least expensive medical services available on the market, we have made it impossible to reign in the growing cost of Health Care.

In 2010, the Federal Budget for health care services in the United States (Medicare and Medicaid) superseded that of Social Security and National Defense. And, as a Nation we now spend nearly 40% more on Health Care -- both public and private -- than any other industrialized democracy in the world. Yet, considering indicators such as general health and life expectancy, we are falling to the rear as one of the healthiest of nations.

The predominating political parties continue to argue the causes of how Health Care has become so expensive. Prompting many to advocate a system of *Universal Health Care*. There are many who are beginning to think: "What the heck! Health Care has always been expensive. Let's just grit our teeth and dig deep into our pockets."

However, the reasons for the unrelenting expansion of the Health Care budget are really plain to see.

First, and most frankly, not all doctors are good. Just as not everyone who plays basketball can make it to the NBA, not everyone who graduates from medical school will make a good doctor. Many people have the impression that "a doctor is a doctor." But that is not true. There is an entire spectrum of physicians, from the "knowledgeable, caring, and astute" to "the flat-out lousy butcher who practices one step away from a malpractice suit."

Second, our educational system is failing to keep pace with other industrialized democracies in graduating a competent and reliable army of industrious and innovative chemical, electrical, and mechanical engineers able to meet the demand for new and reliable diagnostic tools, therapeutic medicines, and medical equipment.

Third, there are patients who have little or no incentive -- under the present system of Health Care -- to be proactive in defense of their own good health. Instead, they rely on healthy Americans -- without benefit of reward for having managed to stay healthy -- to "carry them."

And finally, we have utterly failed at keeping the Health Care industry free of profiteering interlopers who contribute nothing directly to the health of our citizenry.

Despite the sorrowful fate of our First President, the physicians at the bedside of George Washington -- even in their disagreements -- did what they could to save their patient. They made the best use of the limited knowledge and technology of their time. As Dr. Brown said, they were "governed by the best light we had." Each physician sought to cure General Washington, guided solely by their Hippocratic concern for their patient and their patient alone. They saw no need to seek the "assistance" of non-medical personnel, whose interference would yield them no advantage in their search for his cure. The "risk" of allowing such interference would have greatly outweighed the "benefits" to their patient. They would -- without a doubt -- have considered such individuals as nothing more than trespassers seeking to profit from their patient's misfortune. None of those physicians, or George Washington himself, would have tolerated such meddling in the personal affairs of our citizens.

As the world economy becomes global, and as life extension beyond one hundred years becomes likely with the advance of medical science, it is essential that, not only Health Care costs be reduced, but also that Health Care be made available and accessible to all. The preservation and perpetuation of our American way of life depends on a free and healthy, hardworking and innovative workforce!

There are those who argue that Health Care is a "Right." And those who argue that Health Care is a "Privilege." For a nation that could slip from prominence as the richest nation on Earth, Health Care is neither a "Right" nor a "Privilege." For the democratic peoples of any nation -- both now and into the foreseeable future -- who wish to retain their high standard of living in an increasingly competitive world, Health Care is a "Necessity."

In the final chapters of this short work, we will present a model for a Health Care system that can deliver excellent and efficient medical care to the entire American population, while at the same time dramatically reducing the cost of that care.

Fundamentally, this involves the establishment of a unique new form of Health Care: a system in which a *fair and free market* will dominate, a system in which highly competent and compassionate physicians and their patients will be totally in charge of the care of patients, a system that will reward citizens who do their best to stay healthy and allow those in times of need to choose the best providers the industry has to offer.

Chapter 6
The Cost-Drivers of Health Care

****

Abstract

There is little doubt that reducing the costs incurred by poor to mediocre physicians whose overall knowledge of their field, general clinical astuteness and compassion for their patients are wanting, and whose tendency to practice assurance and avoidance behaviors have become routine will result in the enhancement of medical care for all at less cost. There is little doubt that reducing the costs incurred by the designing, engineering, producing, testing and marketing of new and innovative pharmaceutical and medical technology -- costs that can be significantly reduced by effectively improving the quality of our physicians by their return to the mindset and professional practices delineated in the *Hippocratic Oath* -- will result in the enhancement of medical care for all at less cost. There is little doubt that reducing the costs incurred by the ill-informed and less than cooperative population of unmotivated and/or irresponsible citizens -- who consistently fail to act proactively in defense of their own good health -- will result in the enhancement of medical care for all at less cost. And, there is little doubt that reducing the costs incurred by nonessential corporate factions, whose presence in the Health Care industry is of no benefit to doctors or their patients and is -- as a matter of medical practicality -- entirely superfluous, will result in the enhancement of medical care for all at less cost. These facts make the solution to the Health Care Crisis facing America obvious.

****

Before examining the major cost-drivers of the cost of Health Care in America, we need to dispense with another expense that -- in terms of absolute dollars -- pales in comparison to the others. An area of concern that has held an inordinate degree of attention by our politicians, the media and, therefore, the general public for at least the last several decades: namely, *medical malpractice lawsuits*.

If any analyst were inclined to draw a line between the rising costs of Health Care and increased medical malpractice litigation, there would be a direct and clear correlation between the two. It comes as no surprise that a recent issue of *Physician's Practice* magazine featured the following as its lead article: *Bill Like A Lawyer, How To Get Paid For Your Time* (*Physician's Practice*, January 2009, Loma Linda University Medical Center). As physicians are by no stretch of the imagination attorneys, the title of the article expresses a kind of perverse wishful thinking.

Attorneys, like many other professionals, serve clients in the capacity of a consultant, and are usually paid an "up front" retainer that can amount to thousands of dollars. In addition, they charge hourly fees, including fees for phone conferences, billed on a monthly basis. In some cases, attorneys who take cases on a contingency basis don't charge their clients initially for their services. Instead, they take a share of their client's recovered monies, often amounting to 30-50% of compensation awarded for damages suffered.

In contrast, physicians practicing all over America under the existing *vertically integrated managed care system* are paid at a rate decided by insurance companies managing Health Care payments. This means that no matter how many phone consultations doctors may have with a patient, and no matter how many hours they might be required to meet with and examine, diagnose and treat their patient, it is the insurance company that will decide how much their time is worth and how much the physician will be paid: usually amounting to mere pennies on submitted dollar claims.

These same physicians -- who earn an average of $200,000 per year -- also pay an average of $20,000 per year to be represented by legal counsel in the event of a lawsuit against them. That amounts to approximately $20 billion in premiums paid to medical malpractice insurance companies by approximately 1,000,000 American physicians. Malpractice attorneys have an average income of nearly $70,000 per annum and are paid for their services regardless of the outcome of the lawsuit. Hospitals, physicians' groups, and other medical industry personnel associated with the work that physicians perform also pay malpractice insurance premiums amounting to tens of billions of dollars per year.

Any patient, anywhere, at any time, for any reason, can initiate a lawsuit against any medical personnel who have participated in their care. They simply have to log onto the Internet and, within seconds, locate any one of a multitude of attorneys who pride themselves on suing doctors for hundreds, thousands, or millions of dollars. Lawyers will often encourage their clients to include claims for any "special damages" they think juries might be persuaded to consider.

Having taken a case, medical malpractice attorneys will then send a "formal notice of intent" to file legal action against any medical practitioners they deem culpable. After flipping through the hospital records of their client, the letter of intent is sent to every individual and industry entity whose name or identity appears in the medical chart notes. These individuals and firms are informed of their "extreme neglect," "negligence," and "malpractice" regarding said patient. Very often, an individual named in the chart notes is assumed to have been the manager of care for a patient, when in fact they played a lesser role as a consultant in the patient's overall care. These notices are intended to intimidate, frighten, and threaten physicians and their assistants with enormous financial and professional loss. Rather than going to court, however, lawyers first attempt to extort defendants into "settling" the case within 90 days or less, as stipulated by state laws, by paying damages of $250,000 or more to the offended party named in the "notice of intent." Physicians, hospitals, and everyone else named as party to the intended lawsuit find themselves paying considerable amounts in their own legal defense whether or not the case ever goes to court. Despite the reality that all those named in the "notice of intent" have usually done nothing but perform their medical best for their patient; as evidenced by the fact that 90% of all malpractice suits that wind up in court result in physicians being found innocent of all wrongdoing. Yet, those frivolous threats and unsuccessful lawsuits drive up Health Care costs for all of us, in the form of rising malpractice insurance premiums which the medical industry passes on to us: the patients. Including those patients who may have been -- but were probably not -- the victims of bad physicians. As recently as 2008, physicians' advocacy groups estimated that 60% of all malpractice claims against physicians are either withdrawn or dismissed without payment. Still, in those cases that were never adjudicated, the cost of a minimal legal defense averaged $22,000 per case.

More disturbingly, while the total cost of claims awarded malpractice plaintiffs is only several billion dollars annually, the costs incurred by what the *American Medical Association* calls *defensive medicine* may be as much as $120 billion each year.

Defensive medicine is the practice of conducting diagnostic or therapeutic procedures primarily to safeguard against possible malpractice liability rather than to ensure the health of the patient. To reduce their chances of ever having to pay damages in the event of a lawsuit, doctors have been obliged to practice *defensive medicine*. The practice of defensive medicine involves two major physician behaviors: *assurance behavior* and *avoidance behavior*.

Assurance behavior involves the charging of unnecessary services in order to (a) decrease the incidence of adverse low-risk outcomes, (b) deter disgruntled patients from filing medical malpractice claims, or (c) provide physicians with documented evidence that they have used treatments consistent with contemporary standards of care; so that, in the event of legal action the doctor can show that they attempted to preempt any possible liability.

Avoidance behavior is the physician's less than Hippocratic practice of refusing to participate in high-risk procedures, where the risk *vs.* benefit analyses decisions are "too close to call." The risk *vs.* benefit analysis, of course, gives consideration to whether or not the physician is more likely to become a defendant in a malpractice lawsuit for having performed the procedure. Rather than whether or not the procedure -- however risky -- could have benefited their patient. The mere professional act of "making their best call" can put the physician at greater risk of being sued. Avoidance behavior is considered by most medical practitioners to do more harm than good to patients.

The medical community's fear of being sued, especially in emergency, obstetrics, and other high-risk specialty cases, is the driving force behind defensive medicine. The cost of defensive medicine amounts to approximately 4% of the total cost of Health Care in the United States. That is half as much as the total earnings of the one million physicians caring for America's ill. Whereas, the amount paid to plaintiffs in cases where damages were awarded amounted in 2003 to a mere 0.2% of the total cost of Health Care in the United States.

Much of this "sue happy" behavior stems from the belief, on the part of the general public, that the practice of medicine is an exacting science. Therefore, the failure of any physician -- in any case -- must be due to sheer stupidity and incompetence. But the practice of medicine *is not* an exacting science. While physicians must make use of the vast wealth of knowledge gleaned from the physical, chemical, and biological sciences, medicine is -- in actual practice -- more of an art. As in the days of the Founding Fathers, the actions of contemporary physicians are still "governed by the best light."

What most patients fail to understand, but most attorneys understand too well, is that unlike other professions, physicians must proceed in caring for their patient with limited information. The physician's diagnostic and treatment strategies are guided by their training, knowledge of their craft, experience and reasonable judgment. They must continuously juggle multiple and unpredictable variables, adding to that balancing act the fact that no two patients are exactly alike. Disease processes hardly ever follow strict timelines of progression or amelioration. As such, the physician is always taking a calculated gamble, guided by their knowledge and training, experience and judgment, and hopefully their genuine concern for the patient. A patient's outcome depends on many factors, including their underlying health, their particular disease process, the timing of care, as well as the physician's skill. All during the diagnostic and treatment phases, a patient's chances for a healthy outcome is frequently muddled with conflicting facts and alternative choices. The "best light" is usually hazy. Malpractice attorneys, on the other hand, have the luxury of viewing the whole complicated series of physician-patient interactions in hindsight. When it is no longer cloudy, at a time when the physician's actions can be picked apart without regard to why decisions were made at the time they were made.

In a system where little accountability or responsibility is placed on the patient for seeking out and maintaining nominal levels of fitness, and the supply of malpractice attorneys is plentiful, the potential for an escalation in the feeding frenzy called "medical malpractice litigation" is unlimited. Of course, physicians who are properly trained, as discussed in previous chapters, and who are morally and ethically fit to perform as physicians under the *Hippocratic Oath*, should be held fully accountable and responsible for the medical care they deliver. But patients, too, must take full advantage of the wealth of medical knowledge and resources available to them to achieve and maintain maximum health. Only in that way can the informed decisions that patients and their doctors make together, in a mutually accountable and respectful *physician-patient partnership*, become mutually binding.

Medical malpractice claims should be reserved only for those extreme cases, which are relatively few in number, where medical personnel -- entrusted with the care of a sick patient -- have intentionally neglected to provide the most appropriate and best care possible. Of course, such cases can be tragically devastating. But the impact those cases have on the increasing direct medical costs of Health Care do not come close to the costs incurred by the number of cases filed every year by manipulative and greedy legal professionals and their clients.

In their efforts to save money, some health insurance companies and HBO's, such as Kaiser Permanente, have had some success at reducing the costs of malpractice litigation. They have begun to require that patients -- before receiving treatment -- agree to dispute medical care cases before a panel of experts for mediation and any resulting arbitration and settlement. The agreements usually require that disputes be settled in a timely manner, months and not years, to reduce legal costs. In order to help increase the quality of medical services and decrease costs, the agreements stipulate that panels of medical experts base their decisions on whether or not the highest standards of care were upheld for patients, and that decisions are expedited in a timely manner.

In the future, any malpractice settlement models making use of these kinds of agreements -- between patients and physicians, group of physicians, or hospital organizations -- must provide that the individuals comprising the "panel of experts" responsible for mediating and arbitrating malpractice claims be uncompromisingly well-informed. Participants sitting on such panels must be up-to-date with the latest research, delivery of care, and general knowledge of all medical disciplines, including the legal, moral, and ethical dilemmas that accompany each area of care. Like judges in general, they must also be free of all financial and legal conflicts of interest with the parties named in malpractice claims filed before them. Only then can patients be assured of an appropriate recovery for damages in those rare cases of true malpractice. At the same time, the decisions of such panels must equally assure physicians and other medical professionals of protection from predatory malpractice attorneys and patients.

By insuring physicians and patients alike that they will not fall prey to the army of malpractice attorneys bent on making a profit from the unfortunate instances where patient care has failed due to *variable* causes, can the increasing costs of malpractice lawsuits and, more importantly, the practice of defensive medicine be curtailed. For as small an additional cost as frivolous malpractice lawsuits are to our Health Care system, there is the old American maxim that "a penny saved is a penny earned."

Which brings us to the more expensive major cost drivers that plague our Health Care system.

(1) There is the cost incurred by poor to mediocre physicians whose overall knowledge of their field, general clinical astuteness and compassion for their patients are wanting, and whose tendency to practice assurance and avoidance behaviors have become routine.

(2) There is the cost incurred by the designing, engineering, producing, testing and marketing of new and innovative pharmaceutical and medical technology: the preponderate cost of which can be significantly reduced by effectively dealing with cost-driver (1).

(3) There is the cost incurred by the ill informed and less than cooperative population of unmotivated and/or irresponsible citizens who consistently fail to act proactively in defense of their own good health.

And, (4) there is the cost incurred by nonessential corporate factions whose presence in the Health Care industry is of no benefit to doctors or their patients and is -- as a matter of medical practicality -- entirely superfluous.

Our failure to diminish or eliminate these unnecessary expenditures will forever deprive our citizenry of the highest quality delivery of medical diagnosis and treatment at fair and free market prices.

The Costs of Poor and Mediocre Physicians

Our physicians are on the front line. It is they who bear the burden of insuring that *health care* (the maintenance of well-being) is enjoyed by the body politic. It is they who render *medical care* (help provided by trained medical personnel) to our citizenry. It is their professional *service* (a caring, responsive, and altruistic attitude consistent with the intellectual application of the *Hippocratic Oath*) that every patient deserves and expects. It is their basic *medical skills and clinical astuteness* that deter them from making unnecessary, excessive, and costly use of diagnostic and treatment *technology* (imaging/

laboratory tests and pharmaceutical/surgical treatments). It is their knowledge of the medical history of their patient and their direct physical examinations at the office or bedside -- their *ex cathedra* wisdom -- that leads to appropriate and less expensive diagnosis and treatment.

However, it has been estimated that in the current vertically integrated health care environment approximately 10 to 25 cents of every dollar spent on *medical care* (the sum of professional *service*, basic *medical skill and clinical astuteness*, and *technology*) is physician related. While 75 to 90 cents of each dollar is technology-driven (use of diagnostic tools, surgical procedures, and pharmaceuticals). As such, there has been a grossly over-weighted increase in the cost of *medical care* resulting directly from the cost of overused *technology*. It is, therefore, obvious that the more intelligent and proper use of available modern medical technology must lead to a substantial reduction in the overall cost of *health care* that will more accurately -- and cheaply -- reflect the actual cost of *medical care*.

Caring for the well-being of the body politic -- *health care* -- should be equated with the astutely planned, confidently initiated, focused and effectively directed work of the trained, competent, moral and caring physician. When we think of *health care*, the last thing that need come to mind is the application of over-rated, over-priced, over-used and, at times, unnecessary technology and drugs.

The reality is that Health Care in this country can be made much more affordable through the recruitment and deployment of an army of physicians having the highest quality of training, a mien for intellectual honesty and unquestionable ethics, and a heightened sense of morality and altruism. Physicians who are expertly trained in diagnosis and treatment -- who base their diagnoses on their enhanced clinical astuteness and view technology as an aide to their clinical skill and *not as a crutch* or a defense against litigation -- will be less reliant on that technology.

The clinically astute diagnosis and treatment of patients is a faculty that physicians must utilize if health services are to improve at lesser cost. Clinical astuteness is the most integral part of the "service" aspect of delivering high quality medical care. It is both clinically critical and medically mandatory for every physician to understand the limitations of technology and to return to the basic skills (conducting a physical diagnosis and learning their patient's medical history and health habits) espoused by the founding father of modern medicine: Hippocrates.

To repeat: It should be the unstated obligation of every doctor to think, "When in doubt, look at the patient!"

Unfortunately, today's monolithic system of vertically managed care (HMO's, etc.) often fosters less intelligent strategies for delivering medical care. HMO administrators, especially, too often allow doctors to hide their inadequacies and inexperience from themselves and others, thereby fostering a climate of cognitive dissonance. In many cases, young physicians contracted by these organizations are right out of medical school, internship, or residency. Being human, young physicians contracted by vertically managed health care companies find themselves in a "business-driven" environment of conflicting thoughts, beliefs, and attitudes that impacts their decision making skills.

In a country that has the highest technological medical expertise when appropriately applied for diagnosing and treating disease, there are as many as 200,000 patient deaths per year from completely preventable physician treatment and/or medication errors. And those are just the deaths occurring in hospitals where statistics are available. Considering the fact that a single physician error can extend a patient's average hospital stay of several days (amounting to about $20,000 worth of care) to several weeks of more expanded and/or intensive care (amounting to $300,000 or more), the cost of physician errors made by physicians trapped in the vertically integrated health care environment, and their medical assistants, costs our system of Health Care as much as $60 billion per year. It has become more and more likely that a significant number of our fellow citizens will literally die from going to a hospital.

In a system that is no longer a "fee for service" system, poor to mediocre physicians, and the minimally trained physician assistants who aid them, earn their incomes from premiums that we all pay to health insurance conglomerates. Regardless of the types of medical practices to which they belong or the level of medical care they provide. In its present state, the physicians of our contemporary American Health Care system are dependant upon health insurance companies that determine their incomes. As do other Health Care practitioners and technical medical personnel (chiropractors, dentists, dieticians and nutritionists, optometrists, audiologists, pharmacists, etc.). A total income for whom in 2009 amounted to approximately $470 billion: approximately 17% of the total cost of Health Care in the United States of America at that time.

FIGURE 3 on the next page illustrates the kinds if medical practices doing business in America, all of which are contracted with health insurance companies commanding the premiums of America's insured population. Corporations that, unlike other entrepreneurial associations that must keep costs low to remain competitive, have few if any serious competitors to drive down the cost of services: a state of affairs that -- as mentioned in the previous chapter -- results from the inability of government regulators to protect competition in that arena. Whereas, a system set up to promote fair and free competition among individuals and groups of well-trained medical professionals can have no other outcome than the endorsement of high-quality health care -- at lower cost -- by the economic "weeding out" of poor to mediocre medical practitioners.

In addition, the "cognitive dissonance" created in today's distracting "business first" environment would be curtailed. The professional, financial, and emotional demands on the more competent and successful practicing physicians would diminish, allowing them to faithfully implement and practice the intellectual, moral, and ethical standards set forth twenty-four centuries ago in the *Hippocratic Oath*. Patients would naturally gravitate toward more competent medical professionals in favor of less caring and less clinically astute practitioners.

By giving the fair and free market the chance to effectively restore, once again, the choice of physicians, physicians groups and hospitals, to patients -- rather than limiting their choice of medical care options to a short list

FIGURE 3

TYPES OF U.S. PHYSICIAN PRACTICES

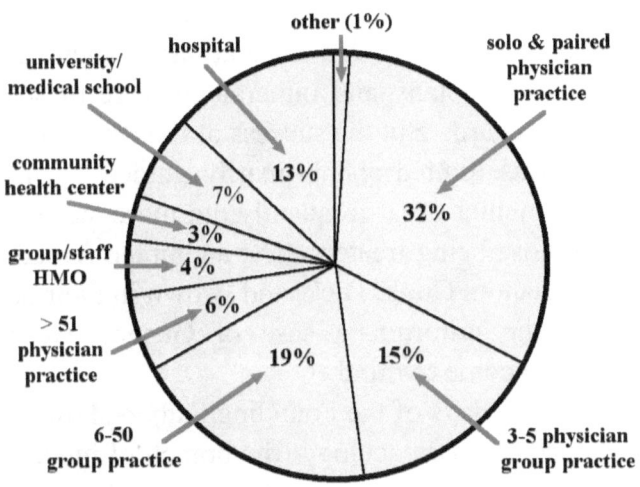

of "insurance provider plans" -- will have no other outcome than the reduction of medical costs due to increased competition among the 1,000,000 practicing physicians and nearly 6,200,000 health care practitioners and medical technical personnel serving America today. With of course, the welcome added side effect of forcing less than competent medical practitioners out of the profession.

The Costs of Necessary But Expensive Medicines and Medical Technology

Despite their training, clinical astuteness and experience, the best physicians must at times make the rational choice to avail themselves of the best medicines and medical technology available in their search for the most fitting diagnosis and favored palliative, surgical, and pharmaceutical treatments.

For millennia, our ancestors have sought cures for what ailed them among the plant extracts and mineral powders prepared from available environmental resources that were close at hand. Their early knowledge of botany and mineralogy were of some use in this regard. But the success of their therapeutic alchemy was limited and primarily guided by trial-and-error methods that frequently did more harm that good to those being treated. The attempted remedies used by Doctors Craik, Dick, and Brown in their handling of the unfortunate case of General George Washington come to mind.

Since the days of the Founding Fathers, however, the science of pharmacology (the branch of medicine concerned with the uses, effects, and modes of drug action) has become a true science. The French physician, Francois Magendie (1783-1855) is sometimes credited with being the "father of pharmacology" for his systematic investigation and isolation of a variety of chemical substances (morphine, quinine, and strychnine). Such substances were in common use at the time in the treatment of a number of debilitating illnesses. And with these new studies, fostered by the

Renaissance and *Enlightenment* which together spawned a new scientific revolution, came the birth of *experimental medicine*: known today as *medical research*. The "father of experimental medicine," the French physiologist Claude Bernard (1813-1878), published the first treatise on the subject in 1865 entitled *Introduction to the Study of Experimental Medicine*. In that book, he described the new field of pharmacology as "the systematic application of experiment in physiology, pathology, and therapeutics to understand health and treat disease."

In the decades to come, the use of the scientific method in the fields of chemistry and biology -- as well as optics that led to the development of more powerful microscopes -- opened the doors to the studies of cell biology, biochemistry, and molecular biology. The experimental approaches of many more scientists were, in turn, adopted by succeeding generations of physicians and scientists who discovered vitamins, hormones, and antibiotics. These discoveries advanced the development of *chemotherapy* (the treatment of disease using chemical substances). Improvements in the art of medicine continued at an accelerated pace, thanks to the invention of more sophisticated research equipment and strategies as well as faster and superior computer technology.

But, as with all progress, there came new costs and controversies. The development of new medication is of vital concern to both medical practitioners and the public they serve. But not surprisingly, that development also has strong economical and political implications.

In the economic sector of our society, the creative developers of new medicine and technology are justified in their expectations to be rewarded for their efforts. While government representatives in the public sector have the obligation and responsibility to " ... *promote the general welfare ...* " under the dictates of the *Preamble to the Constitution*. It is the duty of our elected government officials to make sure that those developers do not intentionally, or through negligence, harm the health of their constituencies. This requires that Congress oversee (read regulate) those innovators through legislation governing the manufacture, sale, and administration of medication. In the United States, the Food and Drug Administration (FDA) is the main body held accountable for the regulation of the pharmaceutical industry, and given the authority to enforce standards set by the *United States Pharmacopoeia*.

The United States Pharmacopoeia (USP) is the official publication of the United States Government containing a list of drugs that can be legally sold in this country, along with their medicinal effects and instructions for use. The *Pharmacopoeia* is the product of the *United States Pharmacopoeial Convention* (a.k.a., USP), a nonprofit organization that owns the trademark and copyright to that publication. All prescription and over–the–counter drugs and health care products sold in the United States are required to follow the standards set by the USP. In addition, it is the responsibility of the *Convention* to provide standards for the ingredients found in our foods and dietary supplements made available for sale.

In the process of developing any new medical product, care must be taken to ensure that the product will do more good than harm, or no harm at all, to the consumer. That endeavor is made all the more difficult, given the complexity of discovering, testing, and manufacturing new medicines and surgical tools and procedures. Despite the many advances made by modern medical science, the complex physiology and chemistry of the human body is still far from completely understood. If it were, there would be a sound strategy for the treatment of every conceivable affliction known to humankind. We are not there yet.

The FDA requires that all approved drugs must be (1) found to be effective against the disease for which approval is being sought, and (2) found to be safe for consumption in extensive animal and human testing. The safety and effectiveness of prescription drugs is regulated under the *Prescription Drug Marketing Act of 1987*. Under that law, all candidate drug compounds must be assessed in a series of metabolic and toxicological studies. And, the study of such compounds is made all the more difficult by the fact that the slightest variation in the molecular structure of a compound can drastically change its effects and effectiveness. Such studies take years and gobs of money to complete!

The development phase of any new pharmaceutical product can take anywhere from a few years to more than a decade and, according to recent studies, may cost between $500 million and $2 billion per drug. It is estimated that of every 5,000 potential new medicines under study only one will find its way to market. To stand a chance of recouping their investment of financial resources, pharmaceutical companies must, first, carefully research the demand for their potential products before spending a dime on development. Then, they must patent their new medicine to insure that the company will profit from their efforts -- for the time prescribed by patent law -- before other companies may legally take advantage of their discovery. Unfortunately, in their ardent efforts to recoup drug-development expenditures, pharmaceutical companies frequently find it to their profitable advantage to use marketing and sales strategies, *in lieu* of ethical judgment, to guarantee earnings following their issuance of new medications. And, many of these tactics have had dire consequences for patients.

Cases of Medicare fraud, appearing recently in the national media, have greatly disturbed the general public: almost as much as the huge salaries and extravagant bonuses awarded to drug company CEO's. These company practices convince the public that many pharmaceutical firms put profit ahead of the welfare of patients. But, it is has been their expensive marketing campaigns that contribute most to the increasing cost of medications put into circulation.

It is not uncommon for us to discover that our physician has been prescribing a new and expensive drug rather than recommending an older and less expensive medicine that can successfully treat the same ailment. Drug companies argue that the steady increases we see in the price of their new products are due to increased demand. When, in fact, such demand is the direct result of a barrage of marketing ploys intended to raise public awareness of these *newer* products regardless of their true potential benefits. All of us have witnessed the continuous bombardment of drug advertisements targeted at potential patient-customers. Customers who are routinely encouraged to "ask their doctor about" expensive new medications: despite the fact that most of these new medications have older generic alternatives that are just as effective. By media brandishing a glut of new brand names before the general public, large pharmaceutical companies, in effect, seek to employ patients as unpaid salespeople for their firms. Brand name medications, in particular, frequently rate an exorbitant markup of as much as 500-1,000%. It is not uncommon for consumers to pay $200 for 100 tablets of a new allergy medicine while the cost of the same number of generic tablets -- having the same active ingredient -- costs $2.

Official representatives of these drug firms, who hardly ever have a science education let alone a medical back-ground, find it effective to provide our medical practitioners with an ulterior motive for prescribing new medications. To boost sales commissions, these salespeople offer "gifts" that sway doctors to prescribe their company's inventory of medications. Although the vast majority of physicians consider these tactics unethical, gifts such as posters and pens, office pamphlets and free samples advertising brand name drugs and their companies are ubiquitous in every physician's office. This tactic amounts to nothing less than an effort on the part of drug producers to influence our doctors' prescription preferences.

A recent study by New York University researchers estimated that the American pharmaceutical industry spends nearly twice as much on advertising than it does on research and development. The pharmaceutical industry's "concern" that we must pay higher prices for their new medications -- because the cost of their research and development projects is so high -- seems misplaced when the industry spent $60 billion on marketing in 2010. The mammoth drug company, Merck & Company, recently spent more advertising Vioxx, (a.k.a., Rofecoxib, Ceocxx, and Ceeoxx), a drug to treat osteoarthritis and other acute pain conditions, than the $125 million spent by the Pepsi corporation to promote their bubbly beverage. The drug, initially approved by the FDA, was later withdrawn from the market over "safety concerns."

Drug company representatives have also had the controversial opportunity to research doctors' prescription records before meeting with them: as doctors are required to keep scrupulously accurate medical reports. With pre-knowledge of a physician's history of the drugs they have prescribed, salespeople find information they can use to persuade physicians to sell more of their company's medicines. While the *New York Times* reported a few years ago that not all doctors have been subject to such "background checks," the American Medical Association recently decided to allow doctors to keep their records off limits to drug sales companies; so that, they can make unbiased prescription recommendations more freely.

Again, it seems that part of the solution to halting the accelerating rise in prescription drugs costs is to stop superfluous outside influences, motivated solely by the incentive for profit, from interfering with the treatment decisions made by doctors and their patients. Decisions that should *only* be made by doctors and their patients and not by clever marketing analysts, persuasive and frequently misleading advertising campaigns, and commissioned drug sales representatives.

It is promising news that more and more patients are starting to shop for generic medications and to buy prescriptions from discount stores to avoid the costs of high-priced, brand name drugs. In addition, doctors and patients should be able to freely purchase drugs manufactured abroad, in cases where *comparative effectiveness research* has shown such medications to be successful. Legislation sponsored by American drug companies to limit such sales ought to be bounced right out of the Capitol Building. The American public deserves the right to purchase whatever will cure what ails them.

Of course, the risks and challenges faced by investors in the pharmaceutical industry are just as endemic to the product designers and developers of the medical technology industry. Like the costs that all Americans incur from the development and distribution of new and effective medications, reducing the costs of developing new and improved medical technology also has its financial and regulatory hurdles.

The "developmental life cycle" of new medical technology includes (1) assessing the need for the new technology, (2) the raw designing and engineering of the technology, (3) the submission of new technology for FDA evaluation of product efficacy and safety, (4) the establishing of standards for the use of the technology for patient care during and following its application, and (5) ascertaining the most cost-efficient and profitable procedures for marketing, distributing, and implementing the use of the new technology to available markets.

Reducing costs in this area will depend a great deal on how well we address the challenges mentioned in the previous section. Training and maintaining an army of compassionate and clinically astute physicians, who behave in accordance with the *Hippocratic Oath*, will surely decrease the use -- and therefore the cost -- of available medical technology. Still, the use of that technology is -- and will continue to be -- a cornerstone of medical diagnostic and treatment strategies.

The major device contributors to the American non-pharmaceutical medical technology market are the CAT, MRI, EKG, and sonogram diagnostic imaging tools. In addition, physicians must frequently avail themselves of cardiovascular procedure technology and in vitro diagnosis technology (biopsy). These technology production sectors, alone, spent more than $100 billion on development in 2005. Other technologies consistently undergoing revision are kidney dialysis technology and orthopedic and invasive surgery equipment technology. In addition, the industry continues to provide the medical care community with consumable supplies from needles and syringes to gauze and tongue depressors.

While drug companies have the luxury of simply changing the name of their merchandise and slapping a new label on the same box of pills -- much like the Kellogg's cereal company changes the face of *Tony the Tiger* on a box of *Frosted Flakes* to boost sales every couple of years -- the medical technology industry is more like the Xerox Corporation. You can't just change the name of a copying machine from the "X500" to the "XX5000," slap a new flashy label on it, and present it as something new: unless of course you have a shrewd marketing "mad man" shilling your wares. A new kidney dialysis machine *must actually do something new or do it a lot better* than the older model! As such, medical technology manufacturing companies are already considering better ways to document and analyze the contribution their technology makes to the medical practitioners and patients that utilize their products.

From the start, it makes perfect economic sense for these companies to maximize the potential value of the technological innovations they introduce to the market. So, medical technology analysts have begun reevaluating the way doctors and hospitals use their equipment with an eye on cost management. They are beginning to assess physician diagnoses and treatment practices against the value of using medical technology in particular medical situations. The unnecessary overuse of medical equipment means increased costs for power, maintenance, repair, and replacement of diagnostic and treatment devices: a practice that can be less cost effective to both the physician-customer and their technology supplier. In addition, medical technology companies are starting to review insurance company coverage plans; so that, patients may be provided with benefit plan options that give them a financial stake in the outcomes resulting from the use of expensive technology. Does a patient who experiences a slight bump on the head really need a CAT or MRI scan? Medical technology developers are beginning to understand that more clinically astute and caring physicians are more likely to make the best call in such matters than the poor to mediocre physicians who practice assurance and avoidance behaviors by default.

Medical technology firms are starting to realize that they and their primary market, medical providers and their patients, can play a significant role in reigning in the costs of new development that can better insure a more profitable return on investment. Medical technology manufacturers know that -- for their industry to survive and profit -- they must create and disseminate product information portfolios that address the value, safety and efficacy of their present and future products. So that, those products can be improved -- when and where necessary -- and put to best use at lower cost.

In an effort to protect their firms from serious financial loss, many of these corporations are beginning to strengthen their partnership with physicians and their patients by listening to both. The result will inevitably be the proper targeting of fewer and fewer investment dollars and the manufacture of only the most necessary products: products that will best serve the needs of future generations of Americans.

The Costs of Poorly Informed, Non-Proactive Patients, And Our Increasingly Aging Populace

In *Chapter 4*, we asked the following question: "Is it possible -- in a nation that has thrived on a fair and free market economy -- to create a cost-effective, efficient, and compassionate Health Care system that manages to *stay in the black* without restricting individual liberties. No matter how foolhardy the liberties taken by the risk takers among us happen to be?"

We are confident that it is. Provided that as individuals we do not interpret the term "liberty" as the occasion to be irresponsible and indifferent to the freedoms enjoyed by our fellow citizens.

The term "liberty" is defined by the *Oxford English Dictionary* as "the state of being free within a society from oppressive restrictions imposed by authority on one's way of life, behavior, or political views." It *does not* define liberty as "the state of being free within a society to do as one pleases at the expense of other members of that society."

The predominating rights and privileges that we all enjoy as Americans are explicitly enumerated in the *Bill of Rights*: the first ten amendments to the *Constitution*. Yet, while the *Bill of Rights* intends for all citizens to enjoy the liberty to pursue their own interests and preferences, it presumes that we will not purposefully or through neglect infringe upon the rights and privileges of our neighbors by acting however we please.

If mistreating our bodies to the point that it affects our health -- whether by personal desire, learned habit, or genetic predisposition -- places a burden on our fellow citizens, it becomes our duty as patriotic Americans to do our best to stop treating ourselves irresponsibly or neglectfully regardless of the inconvenience, effort, or pain that it may cause us.

To solve our current Health Care crisis, it will -- as previously suggested -- take (1) physicians who are knowledgeable, clinically astute and compassionate, (2) a taskforce of scientists and engineers able to design and produce new and innovative medical technology, (3) patients motivated and proactive in defense of their own good health, and (4) the elimination of nonessential parties from the Health Care system. We have already examined the rising costs incurred by the first two imperatives. But, it is the third objective -- the cooperation of "patients motivated and proactive in defense of their own good health" -- that is most essential to the cause of stemming the flow of capital being drained from our economy by that system.

FIGURE 4 shows a list of the approximate costs incurred by the diagnosis and treatment of the major diseases afflicting the American populace.

The annual costs shown represent *direct medical costs* incurred by diagnosis and treatment procedures associated with each given ailment. The *indirect costs* of an illness among those afflicted, as well as those who care for them without compensation, are not shown. Indirect costs have been estimated, in total, to approach anywhere from $200 billion to $650 billion per year. This additional financial loss manifests itself in the form of a more weakened general economy resulting from diminished earnings that decrease spending by both public and private consumers. This

FIGURE 4 ANNUAL COST OF MAJOR DISEASES		
DISEASE	**No. Cases**	**Annual Cost**
heart disease	83,000,000	$ 425,000,000,000
Alzheimer's	5,400,000	183,000,000,000
diabetes	26,000,000	116,000,000,000
influenza	4,000,000	115,000,000,000
hyperlipidemia	100,000,000	100,000,000,000
hypertension	68,000,000	95,000,000,000
arthritis	50,000,000	80,000,000,000
liver disease	30,000,000	80,000,000,000
obesity	116,000,000	75,000,000,000
stroke	800,000	55,000,000,000
cancer	11,100,000	50,000,000,000
Parkinsonism	500,00	50,000,000,000
respiratory disease	62,000,000	34,000,000,000
septicemia	800,000	15,000,000,000
kidney disease	26,000,000	9,000,000,000
TOTAL COST		**$ 1,482,000,000,000**

curtailment leads to fewer sales, less manufacturing and production, and lost tax revenue to the Federal Treasury that might otherwise promote more vigorous private sector production and consumption (more free trade).

It is of particular concern to note that four of the first nine major disease cost drivers are diabetes, hyperlipidemia, hypertension, and obesity: a combination that, as already mentioned, constitutes a medical diagnosis of metabolic syndrome. The reader will also recall that metabolic syndrome is a major contributor to heart disease, which is the number one annual disease cost driver at an exorbitant $425 billion. Together, these five conditions -- diabetes, hyperlipidemia, hypertension, obesity, and heart disease -- amount to a total Health Care expenditure of $811 billion. That is 27% of the $3 trillion cost of Health Care in America. It is just as pertinent to note that obesity is the primary condition that leads to the diagnosis of metabolic syndrome and heart disease.

Obesity now afflicts more than 116,000,000 Americans, a population that constitutes a whopping 35-40% of all Americans between the ages of 4 and 74. An additional 25% of all American adults are considered overweight. The medical community has repeatedly tried to remind us that obesity significantly increases the likelihood of suffering from another four of the major disease cost drivers: stroke, cancer, liver and kidney disease. As indicated above, these latter diseases cost the Health Care system an additional $194 billion. All together, obesity alone is predominantly responsible for costing us more than $1 trillion: or, 33% of the total cost of Health Care in America.

Any hope of sharply reducing the cost of Health Care in America will depend upon the strategies and/or incentives we provide to those individuals who mistreat their bodies out of desire, learned habit, or genetic predisposition to the point that it affects their personal health. Being successful at providing effective health maintenance strategies and incentives for those individuals will radically decrease the number of illnesses mentioned and significantly reduce Health Care costs. In short, such strategies can save the American economy up to $1 trillion per year on Health Care.

One obvious strategy, which is currently being implemented but needs to be more vigorously expanded in both the public and private sectors, is the comprehensive education of our growing and impressionable childhood and adolescent populations. Future generations must be better informed of the medically recommended, healthy life styles they can choose to lead. In addition, the currently overweight and obese adult population of our nation must have access to continuing education on how to improve and maintain good health.

The private sector has been successful -- to some extent -- at providing consumers with dietary programs that can assist them in losing weight and developing better eating and exercise habits. But, many of these companies have also produced a number of "weight loss" products that, unfortunately, consist of nothing more than stimulants (huge doses of caffeine) that reduce appetite and increase energy expenditures than can lead to unhealthful side effects. These products have been shown to have inconsistent and -- at best -- non-lasting weight-loss benefits. We might just as well legalize methamphetamine and cocaine!

Underlying any attempt to assist our obese neighbors to lose weight must be our compassionate consideration that many of the behaviors that lead to obesity are strongly influenced by hard to break personal cravings, family taught eating and exercise habits, and hereditary predilections. Nevertheless, we must also be firm in reminding afflicted individuals that these pressures do not exempt them from their civic obligation to do their best to maintain their own good health as free citizens in an industrious and mutually supportive American social order.

There are also *economic incentives* that can help individuals to modify unhealthful behaviors that do not exist in our current Health Care system. The incentives proposed in the next chapter are an obvious and essential part of the solution to the American Health Care Crisis. Those who already make a habit of practicing healthful behaviors, many of whom considerate it an unfair sacrifice on their part to offer financial incentives to those who practice unhealthful behaviors, can be assured that they, too, will benefit financially from the solution to the Health Care Crisis proposed in *Chapter 7*. That solution will guarantee rewards to those who already act responsibly in defense of their own good health while at the same time reducing the overall cost of Health Care. Up to now, it is our healthy population that has taken on the burden of increasing insurance premiums and Medicare payroll deductions without seeing a return on their investment. It is time our physically fit citizens reaped the benefits of such a return!

Still, there is another reality that must be of concern to every American. And that is the fact that our nation -- until most recently -- has led the world in life expectancy. Because of our past innovativeness, particularly in the areas of scientific and medical research, we are living longer lives. This is a blessing that has brought along with it the curse of increasing Health Care expenditures.

FIGURE 5 illustrates the population of U.S. citizens, 65 years of age and older, by size and percent of the total population between 1900 and 2010 as recently reported by the United States Census Bureau.

As can be seen by the graph, the raw numbers and percent of our elderly population are increasing. Thanks primarily to the miraculous achievements

FIGURE 5
**POPULATION OF U.S. CITIZENS, 65 YEARS OF AGE
AND OLDER, BY SIZE AND PERCENT OF THE TOTAL POPULATION
BETWEEN 1900 AND 2010.**

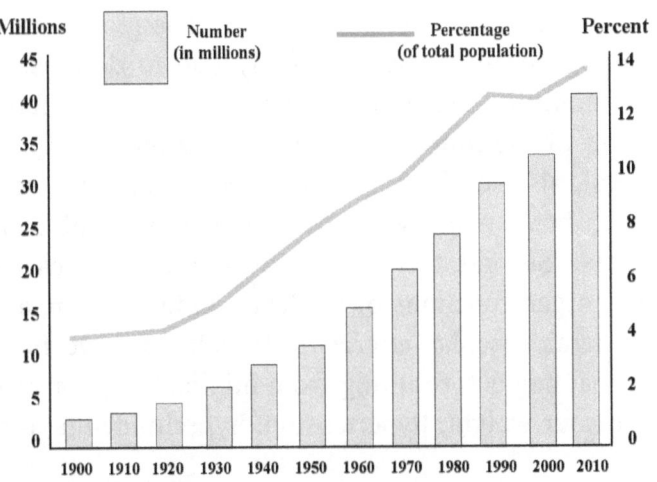

made by our medical research scientists. In point of fact, contemporary scientific journals report the predictions of many respected medical researchers who expect that the secrets of aging will be unraveled within one or two generations! But until our gerontologists succeed in actually solving the age-old mystery of growing old, our citizenry must deal with the social and economic challenges presented by an increasing population of elderly persons whose economic contribution to our society could be consequentially reduced. The solution to the Health Care Crisis proposed in *Chapter 7* will allay any fears that a reduction in the economic contribution made by our growing elderly population will become as significant as some suspect it might be.

All of us are familiar with the minor and major medical complications that take place as we age. First, we become more prone to acute illnesses (the common cold) and experience a delay in the repair and healing time of simple cuts and bruises, resulting in an increased period of recovery. The recuperation of aging bodily tissues is largely due to diminished functioning of the immune system. Reduced functioning of the immune system among the elderly, in general, also results in an increased incidence of leukemia, bone marrow fibrosis, and almost all solid cancers. Second, there is significant wear and tear on major organ functions of the heart, kidney, brain, and peripheral vascular arteries. Which, after years of personal neglect, resulting from minimal to poor control of our weight, hypertension, hyperlipidemia, diabetes mellitus, and arteriosclerosis lead to bodily functions that become all the more hampered.

As the inevitable result of the aging process, two areas of medical care become more and more vital: (1) the early diagnosis and treatment of acute disease, and (2) the aggressive implementation of preventative Health Care intervention strategies that serve to delay -- and evade -- chronically debilitating and deteriorating disorders.

As medical and surgical advances toward the alleviation of conditions such as heart disease and cancer improve at an accelerated rate, the average elderly patient's knowledge of how to live a healthier and productive lifestyle is growing at the same time. As such, we have no idea what the average life expectancy of our children's generation will be. It may sound implausible, but the time may soon come when it is commonplace for the *average* American life expectancy to exceed 100 years. Or, perhaps even 150 years! This is not altogether unreasonable considering the fact that at the end of the 18th Century, at the start of the Industrial Revolution, average American life expectancy was 40 years of age. Medical science has discovered a great deal in the passed 200 years. Today, our average life expectancy is between 75 and 80 years. And the rate at which our scientific knowledge is increasing is growing exponentially. The flip side of this optimism is that the "geriatric population" -- however that population may come to be defined -- may consume a greater portion of our Health Care resources. Should we fail to implement rational measures to belay those prospective costs, our economy and standard of living will suffer. Simply raising the retirement age will hardly be sufficient to solve that potential problem.

With regard to all ages -- young and old alike -- an efficient and inexpensive preventative Health Care system is our best option. Assuming, we expect to remain a free and economically viable society. That system must actively and vigorously encourage and reward the cooperation of citizens who are motivated and proactive in defense of their own good health. An inexpensive, efficiently functioning, helpful and successful system of American Health Care is no longer a "Right," nor a "Privilege," but a "Necessity." That state of mind is as necessary to the survival of our basic freedoms as the *Constitution* that guarantees us those freedoms. Such a mindset can insure that we will do nothing less than guarantee America's place as the most free, healthiest and wealthiest, most influential democracy in the world.

The Costs Incurred By Nonessential Players In Our Health Care System

Imagine yourself in the winter of 1799, hovering unobtrusively like the spirit of Christmas Present, at the bedside of General George Washington and his Doctors Craik, Dick, and Brown. The three doctors, guided by "the best light," are trying to nurture the Former First President back to health. Given the medical knowledge of their time, the three of them debate their diagnoses, considering every curative strategy at their disposal. But their sick friend remains in dire straits.

As Doctor Craik applies a warm poultice to the patient's neck, and Doctor Brown prepares another solution of calomel and tartar, a smartly dressed young man with a quill pen and pages of parchment enters the room. Ignoring the sick man in the bed, he begins scribbling notes as fast as he can, and commences to put questions to them regarding the patient's symptoms, diagnosed ailment, and modes of treatment.

You witness the following bewildering conversation:

STRANGER: Good day, good doctors. My name is Fumblecase. I am ... mmm ... *(glances at one of his parchments)* Mister Washington's private health counselor. May I interrupt you for a moment to ask you a few questions?

DICK: Questions? We're in the middle of ...

FUMBLECASE: Yes, I realize that. But you see. I am required to document and review your actions -- as well as offer any advice you might need -- so that my company can justify payment to your accounts for any services you render on behalf of our client.

CRAIK: Are you a physician?

FUMBLECASE: Heavens, no! But, I can contact any one of our firm's many associates -- who once may have practiced medicine -- to assist us in making the best possible decisions regarding the patient's situation. After all, Mister ... *(glances at his notes again)* ... Washington does pay us a hefty monthly sum to insure that -- in the event of illness -- his money is wisely spent.

The three doctors eye the stranger with incredulity.

DICK: We're not interested in money, sir. We only wish is to make our patient well.

FUMBLECASE: Certainly. But, I have a job to do. So let us begin. What exactly ails the man?

Again, the physicians look at one another and proceed to voice their differing medical diagnoses. They begin to politely argue their respective opinions amongst themselves until the interloper interrupts them.

FUMBLECASE *(waving his quill)*: Excuse me, gentlemen. You seem to have some disagreement as to the status of your patient *(sighs and shakes his head disapprovingly)*. Are you sure there is actually something wrong with him?

*The doctors glance at one another then at
Washington. The First President convulses in
an exasperating heave to take another breath.
The physicians stare blankly at one another
then at Fumblecase who his jotting more
notes.*

BROWN: Are you kidding?

FUMBLECASE *(mumbling to himself as he
writes)*: Probably an upset stomach. *(looks at
the doctors)* Just what have you prescribed
for this ... mysterious condition?

CRAIK: We have bled the patient.

FUMBLECASE: Good ... good. That is covered.

BROWN: We suspect that draining a quarter
of his blood supply will serve to remove any
toxins that have disrupted his balance of humors.

FUMBLECASE: Of course.

CRAIK: We have also applied warm poultices and given him a rectal solution of calomel and tartar.

BROWN: This will cleanse his intestines by
producing an adequate release of the bowels.

FUMBLECASE *(thumbing through several
pages of parchment and reading briefly before*

nodding): Our company will pay for either the calomel or the tartar: but not both.

Again, the physicians glance at one another then stare at the stranger.

FUMBLECASE *(shrugging)*: Very well *(makes another note)*.

BROWN: We have also made him inhale warm vapors of vinegar and water and ingest another ten grains of calomel followed by continued doses of tartar to make him vomit. *(pauses)* Whether or not you pay for it.

FUMBLECASE *(thumbing through more pages of parchment, he reads briefly before shaking his head)*: I am afraid Mister Washington will have to pay for the vinegar as well out of his own pocket. We cannot reimburse him for that.

DICK *(looking at the other doctors)*: I still recommend that we perform a tracheotomy to open the patient's obstructed air passages.

FUMBLECASE (*his eyes opening wide)*: No! No! Absolutely not! That procedure is still experimental. It has not yet been tested on several thousand of our fellow Americans. We have no idea how it might affect him. Don't dare think of such a thing!

Craik and Brown look at Dick.

BROWN *(turning to Fumblecase)*: Doctor Craik and I did express our reluctance to perform that particular procedure.

FUMBLECASE: Thank the Lord! *(mutters to himself)* At least there are two competent surgeons in the room. *(aloud while scribbling)* Would you like me to send a letter to one of our advising former physicians to assist you in agreeing not to perform that procedure?

DICK *(turning to adjust the poultice on the Former President's swollen red neck)*: That won't be necessary.

FUMBLECASE: Very well, then. I shall not take any more of your time. I think I have all the information I need. *(smiling politely)* Don't hesitate to send a horseman if you need us. When our company makes it's decision as to whether or not we can pay you for your help with Mister ... mmm *(glances back at his notes)* ... Washington, we will let him know. It shouldn't be more than a week or two.

DICK: He'll probably be dead by morning: tartar or no tartar.

FUMBLECASE *(turning toward the door having never bothered to lay eyes on the man in the bed)*: So sorry to hear that. *(shaking his head)* He was always very prompt with his premiums.

Fumblecase slams the door behind him as the three physicians stare nonplussed at one another before returning to comfort their patient.

Neither Hippocrates, nor Doctors Craik, Dick, nor Brown would have tolerated an intrusion from the likes of Mister Fumblecase into their patient's bedroom. To them, he would have been nothing less than an absolute nuisance, an irritating distraction, who could do nothing to aid them in their efforts to heal the First President.

Now, recall your latest conversation with any representative of any given health insurance company or your session with their prerecorded automatic response secretaries. Then, ask yourself this simple question: Did they, in any way, play an active role in curing you or your loved one's ailment? Or, were they, instead, a hindrance to your efforts to make sure your doctors were paid in a timely fashion for the services they rendered? So that, you could not be held liable for expenses you thought were covered under your health insurance policy.

Despite the simple fact that such companies do nothing to enhance the medical care provided by millions of hardworking physicians and their medical associates, and simply serve to the pay *bills they decide to pay* under the terms of your convoluted policy, American health insurance firms are among the most profitable corporate interlopers in the world. They are -- in point of fact -- nonessential to the practice of good medicine and nothing more than an exorbitantly high-priced bill paying service.

As previously mentioned, the idea of "health insurance," when first conceived in the 19th Century, may have been a good idea for a fledgling nation whose citizenry needed to "hedge their bets" against disaster in the new age of industrialized machines. But, in today's global economic environment, when America desperately needs a healthy, vigorous, and financially secure workforce, such institutions have outlived their economic utility.

FIGURE 6 is a summary of the TOP SEVEN EARNING HEALTH INSURANCE COMPANY TOTAL PREMIUMS RECEIVED, MEDICAL BENEFITS PAID, MEDICAL OPERATING COSTS, AND PERCENT OPERATING COSTS.

As one might assume in any simple business accounting, **Medical Operating Costs** were construed by the authors to be the cost of administering aspects of the health insurance business strictly related to medical care (time processing claims, administrative and

FIGURE 6				
TOP SEVEN EARNING HEALTH INSURANCE COMPANY TOTAL PREMIUMS RECEIVED, MEDICAL BENEFITS PAID, MEDICAL OPERATING COSTS, AND PERCENT OPERATING COSTS (in millions of dollars for the year 2010)				
Insurance Company	Total Premiums Received*	Medical Benefits Paid*	Medical Operating Costs	Percent Operating Costs
UNITED HEALTH	$ 85,405	$ 68,842	$ 16,564	19%
WELLPOINT	53,974	44,927	9,047	17
KAISER	44,200	40,222	3,978	9
HUMANA	32,712	27,088	5,624	17
AETNA	29,433	24,733	4,700	16
CIGNA	18,393	12,233	6,160	33
HEALTHNET	13,341	11,777	1,564	12
TOTALS	$ 277,458	$ 229,821	$ 229,821	17%

* With the exception of Kaiser Permanente, amounts for Total Premiums Received and Medical Benefits Paid were verified using a variety of sources including *Security and Exchange Commission Form 10-K* filings for the year 2010.

personnel salaries, the purchase and maintenance of office supplies, utilities, advertising, etc.) and was calculated as the difference between **Total Premiums Received** and **Medical Benefits Paid**. **Percent Operating Costs** were calculated as **Medical Operating Costs** over **Total Premiums Received**. According to this data table, an average of 83% of **Total Premiums Received** were shelled out as **Medical Benefits Paid**, leaving 17% of premiums received to be spent on **Medical Operating Costs**.

Of course, insurance companies don't let our premiums sit around in checking and savings accounts earning low yield interest. Like any good investors, they plunge those premiums into Wall Street brokerage houses, hoping to "make a killing" in the market.

FIGURE 7 shows the same TOP SEVEN EARNING HEALTH INSURANCE COMPANY TOTAL EARNED REVENUES AND PROFITS FROM INVESTED PREMIUMS.

FIGURE 7			
TOP SEVEN EARNING HEALTH INSURANCE COMPANY TOTAL EARNED REVENUES AND PROFITS FROM INVESTED PREMIUMS* (in millions of dollars for the year 2010)			
Insurance Company	**Total Earned Revenues***	**Profits from Invested Premiums**	**Percent Profits from Invested Premiums**
UNITED HEALTH	$ 94,155	$ 8,750	10%
WELLPOINT	57,844	3,870	7%
KAISER	42,200	1,978	5%
HUMANA	33,836	6,775	4%
AETNA	31,604	2,171	7%
CIGNA	21,253	2,860	16%
HEALTHNET	13,620	279	2%
TOTALS	**$ 294,539**	**$ 26,683**	**7.3%**

* With the exception of Kaiser Permanente, amounts for **Total Premiums Received** and **Medical Benefits Paid** were verified using a variety of sources including *Security and Exchange Commission Form 10-K* filings for the year 2010.

As shown above, these companies had **Total Earned Revenues** in the amount of nearly $295 billion from which they earned, on average 7.3% profit from their investments. **Profits from Invested Premiums** were calculated as the difference between each companies reported **Total Revenues Earned**, shown in FIGURE 7, and **Total Premiums Received**, shown in FIGURE 6. Health insurance companies assure us that executive bonuses, stock dividends to stockholders (if any), and the administrative costs of running the "investment side" of their insurance business, are paid from gross **Profits from Invested Premiums.** Which seems fair. Since, they should be entitled to the profits they earned for those "services rendered." Services that amount to profiting from the investment of the money they take from our bank accounts (and our employers' bank accounts) to make money on Wall Street while paying some -- but not all -- of our doctor's bills using the money they got from our checking accounts.

Such are the bare-bone-workings of the modern American health insurance industry.

However, the only pertinent question to be considered with regard to Health Care is as follows: What services are health insurance companies providing to aid in the direct medical care of America's citizenry? Answer: None! They are merely a business service whose primary function is to process payments to our physicians for direct medical services rendered by those physicians.

Thank you, very much, Mr. Health Insurance Conglomerate!

Had that money remained in our own checking accounts, totally under our control and quickly-at-hand when we needed it -- *gaining interest for us!* -- we could have written those checks to our doctors ourselves. And, more likely than not, the bill would have been less: perhaps 10% to 15% less due to lower administrative costs!

Practicing physicians and hospitals -- hundreds having declared bankruptcy due to excessive administrative costs -- have estimated that 20 to 30% of their own billing costs (calculating and billing for medical services) are incurred by attempting to coordinate those billing services with health insurance companies who frequently deny those claims altogether.

FIGURE 8 on the next page illustrates the PERSONAL HEALTH CARE EXPENDITURES BY SOURCE OF FUNDS IN THE UNITED STATES FROM 1998-2008. In that graph, the personal health care expenditures of Americans shown amounts to approximately $1.75 trillion. All payments -- including the $290 billion paid by individuals in the form of direct payments and copays to physicians and hospitals and their medical associates -- are recorded, reviewed, disputed, processed and remitted by health insurance corporations. Even payments under Federal and State programs such as Medicare and Medicaid are reviewed by private health insurance companies subcontracted to the government. Federal and State officials, of course, must also be paid to oversee the actions of these companies over which there is little or no regulation due to the *McCarran-Ferguson Act* mentioned in *Chapter 5*. This Federal and State "oversight" of insurance companies adds to the government's cost of expediting claims by doctors and their patients.

Assuming that the several thousand other health insurance companies not among the top seven use 17% of their **Total Premiums Received** to pay their **Medical Operating Costs,** we can expect that the total "medical operating costs" for the American health insurance industry to amount to about $298 billion (17% of $1,750 billion): nearly 66% of the total cost of Medicare in 2008. The solution to the Health Care crisis proposed in the next chapter will propose a way to "streamline" -- and significantly reduces the costs of -- the bill-paying service currently provided by contemporary health insurance conglomerates.

FIGURE 8

PERSONAL HEALTH CARE EXPENDITURES BY SOURCE
OF FUNDS IN THE UNITED STATES FROM 1998 TO 2008

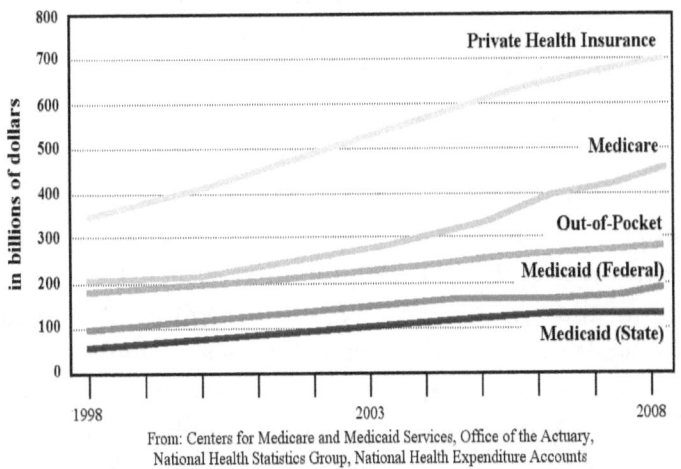

From: Centers for Medicare and Medicaid Services, Office of the Actuary,
National Health Statistics Group, National Health Expenditure Accounts

There is little doubt that reducing the costs "incurred by poor to mediocre physicians whose overall knowledge of their field, general clinical astuteness and compassion for their patients are wanting, and whose tendency to practice assurance and avoidance behaviors have become routine," will result in the enhancement of medical care for all at less cost. There is little doubt that reducing the costs "incurred by the designing, engineering, producing, and testing and marketing of new and innovative pharmaceutical and medical technology" -- costs that can be significantly reduced by effectively improving the quality of our physicians by their return to the mindset and professional practices delineated in the *Hippocratic Oath* -- will result in the enhancement of medical care for all at less cost. There is little doubt that reducing the costs "incurred by the ill informed and less than cooperative population of unmotivated and/or irresponsible citizens who consistently fail to act proactively in defense of their own good health" will result in the enhancement of medical care for all at less cost. And, there is little doubt that reducing the costs "incurred by nonessential corporate factions whose presence in the Health Care industry is of no benefit to doctors or their patients and is -- as a matter of medical practicality -- entirely superfluous" will result in the enhancement of medical care for all at less cost.

In the next chapter, we will present a solution to the health care crisis facing America -- founded on the essence that defines a physician -- that can provide every American and anyone who visits our shores with quality Heath Care at substantially reduced cost.

Chapter 7

*Nothing Less Than a Revolution: A Fair and
Equitable Solution to the Health Care Crisis*

****

Abstract

The solution to the Health Care Crisis facing America requires
that the practice of medicine be returned to a fair and competitive market in which patients can freely choose those physicians
who best suit their needs. By doing so, doctors will be obliged
to render the best possible services at less cost and, in the interest of their own professional survival, become more clinically
astute and discriminating in the use of only the most necessary
diagnostic and effective therapeutic technology in their diagnosis
and treatment of illness and disease. With the creation of individual health savings accounts, which patients may use toward
the purchase of any and all medical services, monies that can
accrue to the financial benefit of patients who live healthy life
styles, individuals will be motivated to become proactive in defense of their own good health; thereby reducing the cost of
treating subacute diseases that contribute to the inevitable onset
of more costly chronic medical conditions. These accounts will
be administered by employees of the Federal Government who
will take no active part in the decisions made by doctors and
their patients but will merely replace contemporary health insurance organizations whose "limited coverage policies and bill
paying services for profit" add unnecessary private and public
expenditures to our current system of Health Care.

****

America has come a long way since the days of
our Founding Fathers. But, the spirit of the American

people -- in good times and bad -- has wavered little. As citizens of a free and democratic society, we cherish the unalienable rights bequeathed to us by our forefathers: the "right to life, liberty, and the pursuit of happiness." And if there is anything that Americans hate more than tyranny it is waste and fraud, which we justly perceive as depriving us of the opportunity to fairly compete with our fellow citizens on a level playing field. Where we all have the same chance of getting "more bang for our buck." It is with these simple ideals in mind, that we can propose a solution to the current Health Care Crisis facing America that can achieve the following objectives:

(1) The attainment of inexpensive and high quality Health Care in the United States of America that is made readily available to rich and poor alike by physicians working in every type of medical practice in the country.

(2) The attainment of inexpensive and high quality Health Care that promotes active and fulfilling lives for all and is regarded as a necessity by Americans who wish to see our nation thrive.

(3) The significant reduction of Health Care costs despite the obstructions of politicians and self-appointed experts who advocate merely throwing more money at the current Health Care system rather than confronting the real challenges that

have, thus far, prevented us from achieving the first two objectives.

As previously discussed, our success at achieving
these objectives will depend upon (a) our capacity to
train and educate physicians able to provide medical
services that promote the highest level of bedside
clinical diagnoses and treatment, (b) our recognition
of the fact that evidence-based diagnosis and treatment are never absolutes and that physicians who lack
the knowledge and/or training to analyze every patient's particular situation tend to drive up costs by
ordering and billing unnecessary tests and procedures,
(c) our ability to educate, and motivate with financial
incentives, a citizenry ready to choose healthy life
styles over unhealthy ones, and (d) our facility to focus our attention on, and target our expenditures at,
physician-patient relationships that exclude business
interests which inflate medical care costs.

Which brings us to our first set of cost-reduction
strategies based on an actuarial analysis of the cost of
medical services provided by captive physicians of
the contemporary vertically integrated health insurance system versus medical providers working as
skilled and clinically astute, caring and compassionate free agents.

As mentioned earlier, the practice of medicine
was once in the hands of physicians who practiced
their trade free of interference from third parties such
as the federal government and health insurance conglomerates. But, in the middle of the 20th Century,
we moved from a *horizontally integrated "fee-for-*

service" system of Health Care to a *vertically integrated system of managed care* directed by health insurance subgroups: health management organizations (HMO's), hospital-based organizations such as Kaiser (HBO's), and private physician organizations (PPO's) contracted to perform services for customer-patients of these organizations.

The decision making process of these health corporations is -- in order to guarantee profits for their stock-holders and executive administrators -- directed from "the top down." Where the practice of medicine is ruled by guidelines set by businessmen whose sole motive is to profit from the misfortune of patients -- by collecting enough money in premiums to "hedge their bets" against losses incurred by those customers who actually became ill regardless of the health care outcome of those customers.

In a vertically integrated system of managed care, physicians have little or no latitude to make otherwise prudent and clinically astute medical decisions that may not go along with the strict courses of action set by individuals whose experience in the field of medicine is frequently limited to their perusal of actuarial charts and profit-and-loss statements. In addition, physicians working for one health care organization are discouraged from seeking the advice or services of other competent physicians working for other health care organizations. In such a system, creative physicians whose sole concern would simply be the health of their patients become more concerned with following the rules of their organization -- for the simple reason that they need to protect their jobs --

and must act to follow those rules regardless of the outcome for patients whom they hardly know. As a result of the transition from a *horizontally integrated "fee-for-service" system* of Health Care, doctors were lured -- out of economic necessity -- to become contractually obligated to a host of private insurance companies. They began treating patients as captive subjects: individuals unable to freely choose their doctor unless those doctors belonged to a particular health network. Since then, patients have no longer had the right to freely choose physicians and hospitals from a ubiquitous pool of truly competitive medical providers. Costs to patients who "go out of network" are artificially increased to punish them for their infidelity. The price-elastic, cost-reduction dynamic of a simple supply-and-demand Health Care system, where patient-consumers can choose the care of any provider-physicians -- doctors forced to compete for those patients by demonstrating a clear and dependable track record of achievement in their field -- has been removed from our economy.

At the core of the cost-reduction strategies made in our proposed solution to the Health Care Crisis facing America is the return to a *horizontally integrated health care system.* A system in which medical practices and organizations do the business of medicine in a fair and unconstrained, competitive market environment that is free of *both* government and politically powerful corporate influences.

In short, physicians and patients must be free to make all decisions regarding medical care; and, payments for all medical services must be under the con-

trol of patients, alone, without government or super-fluous business meddling.

In a system of Health Care in which the choice of physicians is the privilege of patients, competition among doctors better trained in the art of clinical diagnosis and treatment -- doctors who respect and practice the tenets of the *Hippocratic Oath* -- must strive to deliver the best medical care to patients at less cost. Such a system will inevitably drive down costs, and the most talented and efficient medical practices and medical organizations will survive and flourish. Their success, like those of any good business endeavor in a fair and free market economy, will depend upon the ability of talented doctors to develop long lasting and trustworthy physician-patient relationships based on the sound commercial principle of "good will." In such an environment, successful physicians and physicians organizations -- who will train their young "apprentice physicians" straight out of their residencies to embody the same respect and practice of the tenets of the *Hippocratic Oath* -- will, upon their retirement, be able to sell the "good will" of their practices to those equally caring and competent young medical practitioners. This is an exercise that has literally become extinct in the field of modern medicine, today. A practice that is both common to other successful business entities and beneficial to the public whom they have fairly and faithfully served.

To paraphrase a slogan of the pharmaceutical giant, Merck: "Deliver a good product and the profits will come." In a fair and free market, easily accessible Health Care system, delivering the best medical service and care will decrease the cost for those services proportionately. As medical care services and products improve, costs will decrease in accord with the forces of supply and demand.

The failures of the current Health Care system are the product of the unfortunate "side effects" of the *vertically integrated health care organization model.* As these organizations exist today, they have -- from both the provider-physician and consumer-patient perspectives -- effectively eliminated fair and free market competition among medical practitioners. However we look at it, American patients have become captives of "top-down" health care management organizations and cannot "step out of the system" to seek better and less expensive care. This systemic condition makes it possible for doctors to practice "less than the best medicine." In that system, physicians can deliver less than quality medical care -- or no medical care at all -- without regard to the concept of "good will" and with virtually no patient recourse.

By contrast, a horizontally integrated health care system that is open, available, and accessible to all Americans -- regardless of their health status -- has the potential to deliver excellent health care at much lower cost. In such a system, in defense of their own professional survival, physicians will be forced to choose associates they hold in highest regard -- who possess skills based on training, level of empathy, clinical acumen, etc., and reserve only the most essential referrals to those medical professionals having a clear and uninterrupted track record of success. In such a system, patients will be able to choose physicians they feel are best suited to their needs.

Furthermore, physicians in a free and fair, horizontally integrated health care system will find it to their advantage to better serve their patients and educate their protégés by explaining their diagnostic strategy. They will be obliged to teach how and why they diagnose and treat in the manner they do in order to achieve the most healthful outcomes. The vast databases we call the "Internet" can be put at the fingertips of patients seeking the best care, where the performance ratings of doctors and their organizations can be made public by respected scientific and medical associations. Supply and demand will do the rest by assuring that the best doctors remain in the system, that the worst doctors are eliminated from the profession, and that patients are able to seek and receive the best care available. In that regard, patients will have to rely on their own resourcefulness -- and best judgment -- rather than convoluted insurance policy guidelines and restrictions that put corporate profits ahead of patient care.

Why is it that we cherish and unleash our "free market economy" in every field of trade in America other than the field of medicine? Perhaps, it is because we are barred from doing so by both government and private corporate players who wish to retain the *status quo* for personal gain instead of breaking new ground for the benefit of all.

In 2008, according to FIGURE 8 on page 151, our insurance companies (along with federal and state organizations that subcontract the services of those insurance companies) processed $1.75 trillion in medical claims and copays. One can assume that that figure has inflated since 2008. So, had the rising price of health care services increased at a modest rate of 6%, we can calculate the "total personal health care expenditure by source of funds in 2010" to be approximately $2.167 trillion ($1.75 x 1.06 x 1.06). That would amount to $6,567 being spent annually on their health care by every man, woman, and child in America: population, approximately 330,000,000 citizens.

It is repeated *ad nauseam* that more than 40,000,000 persons in the United States "do not have Health Care." That is, of course, an untruth. Since, any person living in America, regardless of their legality, can walk into any hospital in America and receive treatment under the care of any one of millions of medical providers. The reality is that everyone in America already has access to medical care. Therefore, our real concern -- without all the political smoke and mirrors -- is how to deliver consistently better medical care at reduced cost.

One solution proposed by politicians and health insurance companies suggests medical care costs be reduced by simply reducing the amount paid to medical providers (doctors, physicians assistants, nurses, hospital staffs, pharmaceutical and medical technology companies, etc.). Arbitrarily reducing anyone's fees for services rendered is not likely to promote better service. In addition to hating tyrants, waste and fraud, American workers loathe being cheated! Health Care providers are not likely to take such a proposal seriously: even in the face of the ludicrous argument that they would be "doing it for the good of society."

The solution to the Health Care Crisis facing America must be fair-minded and bold, clearly defined, and user-friendly for both providers and patients. A new system of Health Care must emphasize more efficient and less expensive treatments for acute diseases -- by clinically astute and diligent physicians -- that will reduce the incidence of subacute diseases that develop into chronic diseases.

You will recall that obesity now afflicts more than 116,000,000 Americans and that an additional 25% of all American adults are considered over-weight. This single subacute condition significantly increases the likelihood of suffering from diabetes, hypertension, hyperlipidemia, heart disease, stroke, cancer, liver and kidney disease. These diseases alone amount to as much as $1 trillion in annual Health Care expenditures.

The four actuarial analyses that follow are composite examples extrapolated from a variety of resources and include data from 2005 through 2008. The case scenarios presented include situations in which there is (Case 1) inadequate differential (alternative) diagnosis despite the ordering of unnecessary tests to satisfy assurance (legal) considerations, (Case 2) side-effects and/or complications associated with treatment, poor awareness and condition recognition, resulting in follow-up complications, (Case 3) extended hospitalization periods and/or re-hospitalization periods resulting from inadequate antibiotic therapy, and (Case 4) failure to anticipate and prevent a nosocomial (hospital acquired) venous thrombosis and pulmonary embolus resulting from a brief hospital stay for pneumonia.

In perusing these case studies, it is important to reflect upon and judge the impact on health outcomes and medical care expenditures resulting from the care of the previously highlighted acute, subacute, and chronic diseases that afflict our Nation.

Firstly, in cases of acute diseases, it is plain to all those who practice medicine that the primary outcome that any particular acute disease has on a patient depends on the astuteness of the physician and not on the "will of the patient." A person may become acutely ill for a host of reasons (trauma, infection, or other inflammatory conditions). And their recovery, including timeline, scale of recuperation, and the overall cost of cure depends upon the skills, clinical astuteness, motivation and conscientiousness of the physician. The patient's efforts in the cause of getting well -- outside their seeking the best medical care and following their physician's instructions -- have much less impact.

Secondly, in cases of subacute and chronic diseases, the primary outcome that particular diseases will have on a patient depends on that patient's ability to be motivated and proactive in defense of their own future health as well as their capacity to behave in ways that make preventative medical care a personal habit. In the case of subacute and especially chronic diseases, the physician's overall actions have less impact on the patient's outcome. As mentioned earlier, as little as 12% of the cost of chronic diseases can be attributed to the clinical astuteness, skill, and knowledge of the physician. With, of course, the exception of the physician's guidance and reassuring influences once diagnosis and treatment of the primary subacute disease is provided. This "guidance and reassuring" behavior must begin prior to the patient's progression to more chronic, extremely debilitating and often lethal end-stage disease conditions: diseases such as heart, lung, colon, liver, and kidney disease that incur the majority of the cost for all categories of chronic disease.

The four different case examples presented below illustrate Health Care costs indicative of medical care in America. As previously mentioned, almost all physicians in America are well trained in those qualities essential to the practice of medicine: intellect and astuteness, medical knowledge, skill and experience, compassion, patient empathy, etc. However, because they are placed in the precarious position of practicing medicine as captives of vertically integrated Health Care organizations, physicians must practice medicine in an assurance, litigious avoid-ance, and rushed medical environment that short-changes genuinely effective medical care and sabotages the doctor-patient relationship. Because of that rushed and partitioned practice of medicine, health care providers often have follow-up sessions with patients they hardly know or have never seen before: a situation that can promote errors and increased medical expenses. In these four different case examples, standard medical care practices and costs in America are contrasted with the kind of medical services costs that would be provided in a horizontally integrated Health Care system by fair-and-free-market-driven physicians possessing the essential qualities necessary to practice and deliver outstanding medical care. Physicians who are able to professionally demonstrate the behavioral qualities they were taught as evidence of their astuteness as Health Care providers having a strong commitment to the *Hippocratic Oath*, and an unwavering observance of the art and science of medicine.

Case 1 - Acute Diverticulitis

A fifty year-old male patient experiences the sudden onset of left lower quadrant abdominal pain with constipation. After 24 hours, he seeks medical attention at the emergency room. History is significant for continuous left lower quadrant abdominal pain with no prior history of colonoscopy. Direct and rebound tenderness of the lower abdomen are present upon physical examination. The stool on visual rectal examination is heme-positive for occult blood. The patient completed his yearly examination two weeks prior to this illness with normal blood counts, no medication allergies, and his physician's orders to seek out a gastroenterology consultation for a colonoscopy. The patient is not severely ill (no chills, fever). However, the abdominal pain is severe enough to affect normal daily routines, and the rebound tenderness is indicative of an inflammatory process.

In almost any vertically integrated health care setting (HMO, HBO, PPO), today, the emergency room physician's next steps (consultation cost = $325) would include the following investigations and treatments: an abdominal and pelvic CT scan with oral and intravenous contrast (cost = $1,220), blood and urine tests (cost = $360), surgery consultation (cost = $325), intravenous antibiotics (cost = $450), out-patient consultation with a specialist the next day (cost = $325). TOTAL COST = $3,005. The patient is advised to follow through on their consultation with a gastroenterologist for a colonoscopy.

To a well-trained, clinically astute physician working in a horizontally integrated health care system, the obvious diagnosis is *acute diverticulitis*: an infection of the small pouches or sacs of the colon along with constipation. After the initial consultation (cost = $325), the astute emergency room physician working in a free-and-fair market medical system prescribes treatment with antibiotics to reduce the infection such as Flagyl (cost of 20 pills @ 500 mg = $40) and Cipro (cost of 20 pills @ 500 mg = $50) twice a day until symptoms disappear. TOTAL COST = $415. The patient is instructed to contact his personal physician's office the next morning. A blood work-up will be scheduled if -- and only if -- symptoms become worse or do not dramatically diminish within 24 hours. Very close contact and follow-up between physician and patient are strongly recommended. The patient is also advised to follow through on their consultation with a gastroenterologist for colonoscopy after recovery from acute diverticulitis.

TOTAL COSTS FOR DIAGNOSIS AND TREATMENT OF ACUTE DIVERTICULITIS

Vertically Integrated Health Care System Costs		Horizontally Integrated Health Care System Costs	
consultation	$ 325	consultation	$ 325
CT scans	1,220	antibiotics	90
lab tests	360		
surgery consultation	325		
antibiotics	450		
specialist consultation	325		
TOTAL COST (V)	**$ 3,005**	**TOTAL COST (H)**	**$ 415**

SAVINGS TO THE PATIENT

Cash Savings:	$V - H = \$2,575$
Percent Cost Reduction:	$(V - H) \div V = 0.86 = 86\%$

Savings to the patient under the care of the clinically astute physician, working in a horizontally integrated health care model, over the physician working in a vertically integrated health care model is $2,575: an 86% cost reduction.

Case 2 - Crohn's Colitis

A fifty-three year-old male patient with Crohn's colitis (an inflammation of the colon resulting in lower abdominal pain, bleeding from the bowel, and bouts of diarrhea) undergoes a colonoscopy by a gastroenterologist (cost of physician and facility = $3,500). It is completed at 4 pm on a Friday. Upon discharge from the surgery center, the patient has abdominal pain that he reports to the nurse.

In almost any vertically integrated health care setting today, nurses are likely to consult the physician readying to perform their next colonoscopy. The patient is informed that their discomfort is unusual and that the physician who performed the procedure may want to see them and order an abdominal pelvic CT scan. However, nowadays doctors are frequently too busy, emotionally distant and unattached to patients; and, therefore, may never get to see them. The patient returns home and has continuous generalized abdominal pain the entire night but is unable to contact his gastroenterologist. By noon on Saturday, 20 hours after the procedure, his abdominal pain is severe enough for him to visit an emergency room. Approximately 24 hours after the colonoscopy, an abdominal and pelvic CT scan (cost = $1,220) has shown free air consistent with a colon perforation. Following surgery consultation (cost = $325) the patient undergoes surgery (cost of corrective surgery = $31,000). The surgeon performs a right hemicolectomy (excision of the right colon) with a colostomy (opening from the large intestine to the skin) and an ileostomy (opening in the small intestine to the skin). Four months and two surgeries later (cost of additional surgeries = $31,000), the patient is discharged from the hospital (cost of hospital stay at $7,000 per day = $840,000). TOTAL COST (all medications included) = $907,045.

To a well-trained, clinically astute physician working in a free-and-fair market, horizontally integrated health care system -- a physician who is familiar with his patient's history and prior treatments --

the perils of performing a colonoscopy on a patient with severe Crohn's colitis are apparent. Although perforations occur with invasive patient investigations of this kind at a frequency of about 1 in 1,000, primarily in those patients with prior disease, it is in the interest of the patient to remain under observation following his colonoscopy. Complications resulting from these investigations can be quickly diagnosed with an abdominal CT scan and rapidly treated within four to eight hours of the procedure followed by a hospital stay of one week. When treatment is prolonged for as long as 24 hours, however, complications are aggravated and both treatment and recovery are usually longer than two months, assuming the patient does not die. The patient is still under observation when he begins to complain of abdominal pain. The physician orders an abdominal and pelvic CT scan (cost = $1,220) that shows free air consistent with a colon perforation. Following surgery consultation (cost = $325) and surgery to repair the perforation which has not had 24 hours to aggravate the overall condition of the colon (cost = $20,000), the patient remains in the hospital for further observation for an additional seven days (cost of hospital stay at $7,000 per day = $49,000). TOTAL COST (all medications included) = $74,045.

As illustrated in the summary chart on the next page, the savings to the patient under the care of the clinically astute physician, working in a horizontally integrated health care system in the worse case scenario presented, over the physician working in a ver-

tically integrated health care system, is $833,000: a
92% cost reduction.

**TOTAL COSTS FOR DIAGNOSIS AND TREATMENT OF
COMPLICATIONS OF PERFORATED COLON IN PATIENT
WITH CHRONIC CROHN'S COLITIS**

Vertically Integrated Health Care System Costs		Horizontally Integrated Health Care System Costs	
colonoscopy and facility $	3,500	colonoscopy and facility $	3,500
CT scans	1,220	CT scans	1,220
surgery consultation	325	surgery consultation	325
corrective surgery	31,000	colon repair	20,000
additional surgeries	31,000	hospitalization	49,000
hospital stay	840,000		
TOTAL COST (V)	**$ 907,045**	**TOTAL COST (H)**	**$ 74,045**

SAVINGS TO THE PATIENT

Cash Savings:	**V - H = $ 833,000**
Percent Cost Reduction:	**(V - H) ÷ V = 0.92 = 92%**

Case 3 - Acute Appendicitis

A thirty-eight year-old female patient experiences
abdominal pain, nausea, and vomiting for 24 hours.
In the last 12 hours, her temperature has slowly risen
to 101 degrees. She is extremely nauseous and vomiting.

In almost any vertically integrated health care
setting, today, her primary care physician's nurse in-
structs her to report immediately to the emergency
room. In the emergency room, the attending physician
(cost = $325) orders a blood test (cost = $75) and pelvic CT scan (cost = $1,220). The CT scan is incon-
clusive but the blood test confirms her WBC (white
cell count) to be over 19,000 (normal < 10,000). The
abnormally high WBC suggests that the patient's ap-
pendix may have already become perforated, a condi-

tion that leads to peritonitis (infection of the membrane linings covering organs of the abdominal cavity). Following surgery consultation (cost = $325), she is treated with an appendectomy and primary closure of the surgery site (cost of surgery = $10,000). She is hospitalized and intravenous antibiotics are prescribed for 5 days. After 2 days (cost @ 7,000 per day = $14,000), the patient has no fever and a normal WBC. She is discharged with a 5 days supply of Flagyl (cost of 2 pills per day for 5 days @ 500 mg = $20) and Levaquin (cost of 1 pill per day for 5 days at 500 mg = $25). The patient is asymptomatic for more than a week before continuous right lower quadrant abdominal pain begins, accompanied by a temperature of 102. The patient is taken to the emergency room by her spouse, and is re-hospitalized. Attending physicians do a blood workup (cost = $1,000) and imaging studies (cost of CT scan = $1,220; cost of sonogram = $400), and prescribe intravenous antibiotics (cost = $200). After consultation (cost = $325) attending physicians diagnose an abdominal abscess secondary to inadequate post-hospital discharge antibiotics. The patient should have been treated with postoperative medications for at least 2-4 weeks. A CT scan guided percutaneous abscess aspiration (insertion of a tube underneath the skin to drain the collection of pus) and a drain is put in place to remove residual infectious material. The patient requires an additional week of hospitalization (cost @ $7,000 per day = $49,000) before being discharged, and is treated with antibiotics for an additional 6 weeks (cost = $600). Two additional CT scans (cost of scans

@$1,220 per scan = $2,440) two weeks apart are performed to make sure the infection has not reoccurred. TOTAL COST OF INITIAL AND SECONDARY MEDICAL INTERVENTION HOSPITALIZATIONS = $80,850.

To the well-trained, clinically astute physician working in a free-and-fair market, horizontally integrated health care system, the classic symptoms of appendicitis are clear and the patient is instructed to go to the emergency room. At the hospital, the emergency room physician confirms (consultation cost = $325) the family doctor's diagnosis with a blood test (cost = $75) and pelvic CT scan (cost = $1,220). Although, the CT scan is inconclusive, the blood test confirms her WBC count to be over 19,000. Following surgery consultation (cost = $325), she is treated with an appendectomy and primary closure of the surgery site (cost of surgery = $10,000). She is hospitalized and intravenous antibiotics are prescribed for the duration of the patient's hospital stay. After two days in the hospital (cost @ 7,000 per day = $14,000), the patient has no fever and a normal WBC. She is discharged with a 4-6 week supply of Flagyl (cost of 2 pills per day for 35 days @ 500 mg = $280) and Levaquin (cost of 1 pill per day for 35 days at 500 mg = $375) and instructions to immediately report any re-emergence of symptoms. She is to report to the lab once per week for four weeks (cost @ $75 per blood test for 4 tests = $300). TOTAL COST OF MEDICAL INTERVENTION AND HOSPITALIZATION = $26,900.

TOTAL COSTS FOR DIAGNOSIS
AND TREATMENT OF ACUTE APPENDICITIS

Vertically Integrated Health Care System Costs		Horizontally Integrated Health Care System Costs	
consultations	$ 650	consultations	$ 650
blood tests	1,075	blood tests	375
CT scans	4,880	CT scan	1,220
sonogram	400	surgery	10,000
surgery	10,000	hospital	14,000
medicatrions	845	medications	655
hospitalization	63,000		
TOTAL COST (V) $	**80,850**	**TOTAL COST (H)**	**$ 26,900**

SAVINGS TO THE PATIENT

Cash Savings: V - H = $ 53,950
Percent Cost Reduction: (V - H) ÷ V = 0.67 = 67%

Savings to the patient under the care of the clinically astute physician, working in a horizontally integrated health care system, over the physician working in a vertically integrated health care system, is $53,950: a 67% cost reduction.

Case 4 - Deep Venous Thrombosis and Pulmonary Embolus

A morbidly obese, forty-two year-old male (BMI 39.4 - normal < 25.0) is diagnosed with pneumonia by his primary care physician.

In almost any vertically integrated health care setting, today, the primary care physician (cost of consultation = $325) would send their patient to the hospital. Arriving at the hospital, the patient has a temperature of 101 and a WBC of 21,000 (normal < 10,000). The patient is treated with antibiotics and within 24 hours feels better and is ready for discharge the following morning. Before being discharged, however, the patient complains of severe right-upper thigh pain and tenderness. Following consultation (cost = $325), an attending physician orders an ultrasound-Doppler (sonogram) of the right leg (cost = $500) and a ventilation-perfusion lung scan (imaging technique used with isotopes to evaluate the circulation of air and blood within a patient's lungs; cost = $1,000). Physicians at the hospital identify an upper leg, deep venous thrombosis, or DVT (formation of a blood clot in a deep vein) and a pulmonary embolus, or PE (a blood clot in the lung). Anticoagulants with intravenous heparin are administered during the patient's additional 5-day hospital stay (cost of seven days hospitalization @ $7,000 per day = $49,000). Upon release from the hospital, the patient is treated with oral doses of Coumadin for 6 months (cost of 3 pills per day for 180 days @ 10mg = $270) and monthly lab tests to determine prothrombin times (a test to measure the speed and activity of blood coagulating factors; cost = $1,200) and other coagulation indicators. TOTAL COST OF MEDICAL INTERVENTION AND HOSPITALIZATIONS = $52,620.

To a well-trained, clinically astute physician working in a free-and-fair market, horizontally integrated health care system, who has been treating the patient for the usual complications arising from obesity (including poor circulation), the diagnosis of pneumonia dictates special treatment (cost of consultation = $325). Anticipating that his patient will need to spend two or more days in the hospital while being treated for pneumonia, the physician takes preventative measures to preclude the formation of a deep venous thrombosis likely to precipitate a pulmonary embolus in their patient. The patient is treated with antibiotics as well as Lovenox or other anticoagulants. The patient is to wear compression-support stockings and is ordered to get out of bed and walk several times a day during their hospital stay. These standard evaluative prescriptions for DVT and clot prophylaxis (prevention) are likely to prevent the development of these two life-threatening conditions. Within 48 hours the patient feels better and, by direct physical examination, shows no sign of circulatory problems. They are discharged from the hospital after 3 nights (cost of 3-days hospitalization @ $7,000 per day including medication = $21,000). TOTAL COST OF MEDICAL INTERVENTION AND HOSPITALIZATION = $27,325.

TOTAL COSTS FOR DIAGNOSIS AND TREATMENT OF DEEP VENOUS THROMBOSIS AND PULMONARY EMBOLUS

Vertically Integrated Health Care System Costs		Horizontally Integrated Health Care System Costs	
consultation	$ 650	consultation	$ 325
hospitalization	49,000	hospitalization	21,000
sonogram	500		
v-q imaging	1,000		
medications	270		
blood tests	1,200		
TOTAL COST	**$ 52,620**	**TOTAL COST**	**$ 27,325**

SAVINGS TO THE PATIENT

Cash Savings: $V - H = \$ 25,295$

Percent Cost Reduction: $(V - H) \div V = 48 = 48\%$

Savings to the patient under the care of the clinically astute physician, working in a horizontally integrated health care system, over the physician working in a vertically integrated health care system, is $25,295; a 48% cost reduction.

These cases are not exaggerated. Physicians see thou-sands of patients like these every day. The reader is urged to recall that in a nation that has the highest technological and medical expertise in the world, there are still as many as 200,000 patient deaths per year resulting from preventable physician treatment and medication errors: a figure that does not include those millions of patients who had "near death experiences" resulting from treatment and medication errors while in the hospital. In addition, it is pertinent to note that such errors extend patient hospital stays from several days to weeks, and that these prolonged visits frequently include expanded -- or intensive -- care that costs us hundreds of billions of dollars per year. In the vast majority of these cases, the mistakes and misjudgments made by physicians are the outcome of a fuzzy decision-making process, resulting from a kind of "cognitive dissonance" generated by distracting legal assurance and avoidance considerations (fear of malpractice lawsuits) as well as fiscal concerns (insurance guidelines and payment policies). These considerations are continually mulled over by medical practitioners confined to, or contracted by, rigidly organized, vertically integrated health care organizations and institutions.

How many of our citizens would be spared the pain of unnecessarily long hospital stays -- and how much money could our economy save -- if clinically astute, competent, and compassionate physicians working in a horizontally integrated health care system were empowered to act free from these mind-numbing reflections and deliberations? How much would the medical care of our Nation improve *if the sole preoccupation of physicians were their patients*?

In addition to these cases, similar calamities occur -- as part of the *status quo* -- when physicians and patients trapped in a vertically integrated health care system overlook preventative actions that must be taken with regard to other diseases. While it is only fair to mention that a few institutions -- such as Kaiser Permanent -- have tried to expand their preventative health care measures, their efforts to make preventative medical care strictly routine, and to motivate their memberships to be more proactive in defense of their own good health, are still grossly inadequate.

In a horizontally integrated health care system, on the other hand, designed to give patients a "financial incentive" to take preventative health care measures, and in which such measures are viewed as a regular necessity by patients and physicians alike, preventative cancer screening with colonoscopy and cervical pap smear, for example, could almost completely eliminate the onset of the overwhelming majority of colon and cervical cancers. Other investigations such as mammogram, chest x-ray, transvaginal ultrasound, PSA, fecal occult blood, laboratory and urine analysis -- utilized as *mainstream preventative* screening tests (for breast, lung, ovary, prostate, esophagus, stomach, small intestine, kidney, and urinary bladder) would precipitously reduce the number of cancer cases we see each year. Such routine preventative measures are as indispensable to the practice of medicine as the contents of that "little black bag" once carried on home visits by doctors "in days of old," and would sharply reduce the incidence of grave illnesses and the costs they presently incur.

In brief reprise of FIGURE 4 in Chapter 6, take a glance at FIGURE 9 titled ANNUAL COST OF MAJOR *PREVENTABLE* DISEASES.

FIGURE 9

ANNUAL COST OF MAJOR *PREVENTABLE* DISEASES	
Disease	**Annual Cost**
heart disease	$ 425,000,000,000
diabetes	116,000,000,000
influenza	115,000,000,000
hyperlipidemia	100,000,000,000
hypertension	95,000,000,000
liver disease	80,000,000,000
obesity	75,000,000,000
stroke	55,000,000,000
cancer	50,000,000,000
respiratory disease	34,000,000,000
kidney disease	9,000,000,000
TOTAL COST	**$ 1,154,000,000,000**

We have already noted our concern that, in addition to cancer, seven of the fifteen major diseases -- heart disease, diabetes, hyperlipidemia, hypertension, liver disease, stroke and kidney disease that frequently occur as the result of obesity -- cost the American economy nearly $880 billion. Add to that the cost of treatment for obesity and the total becomes $955 billion. Add to these direct medical costs the $50 billion in costs for cancer treatment (malignant and benign neoplasm), as well as the $116 billion cost of influenza contracted by patients who -- for whatever reason -- failed to get inoculated against infections, plus the $34 billion cost of respiratory diseases due largely to smoking, and the total direct medical cost of the major *preventable* diseases that afflict Americans rockets to $1.154 trillion.

Now, add to that $1.154 trillion the cost of *indirect* losses to the overall economy -- estimated to be about $425 billion (in lost wages due to illness among those afflicted plus those incurred by the people who care for them) -- and the accrued financial wilting of the American economy rises to a staggering $1.579 trillion. That is more than half the total cost of Health Care in the United States.

Much of the remaining cost of Health Care is spent by individuals in over-the-counter expenses tending their everyday sniffles, stomachaches, headaches, cuts-and-bruises, or on the researching and development of new and effective medical technology and pharmaceuticals. As mentioned previously, the cost of the research and development of new technology would also drop precipitously if more clinically astute physicians ordered only those tests and treatments that were absolutely necessary.

This profligate frittering away of wealth leads, further, to the curtailment of sales and business revenue which reduce the incentive to manufacture, market, and distribute goods, thereby diminishing tax revenue to the Federal Treasury. Revenue that could otherwise promote more vigorous trade in the public and private sectors.

Now, imagine that our current system of vertically integrated health care -- where the kind of "dissonant thinking" described above is ubiquitous -- was replaced by a fair and freely competitive, horizontally integrated health care system in which "good willed" physicians regularly encouraged their patients to value preventative health care as a measure that would enhance their *long term accumulation of wealth*. A system in which patients who live fit lifestyles, and spend less on medical care, reap financial savings resulting from their healthy behavior.

How much could we save by shifting the mindset of physicians and patients from a "vertically" to a "horizontally" integrated Health Care environment?

Should we conservatively ascribe savings to patients resulting from proactive and preventative medical measures -- taken under the care of clinically astute physicians working in a horizontally integrated health care system -- to a mere 20% of that spent under the existing vertically integrated system, we could achieve an annual reduction of nearly $316 billion in medical costs (0.2 x $1.579 trillion). This is not outside the realm of possibility considering the savings realized in the four case comparisons presented above. Especially with respect to the treatment of subacute diseases destined to become chronic. The staggering amount of $316 billion dollars is an annual savings of $958 for every man, woman, and child in America: a savings of $3,832 for every family of four. An amount of cash that is enough to afford a down payment on a new home within 3-5 years, several months mortgage per year in the years that follow, as well as a little pocket change to stimulate the economy.

America could not ask for a more rational "stimulus package!"

Given the fact that the cost of preventative health care pales in comparison to the costs associated with belated treatments for subacute and chronic diseases, it is reasonable to expect that the actual savings to patients, and the American economy, resulting from our transition from a "vertically" to a "horizontally" integrated health care system, could amount to more than 30%.

This transition would also significantly reduce the cost of administering a health care system that has become seriously "infected" by business organizations that do nothing to aid in the medical treatment of patients and more frequently interfere with that aid. Organizations that tend to overburden physicians and patients with remittance disputes and mountains of unnecessary paperwork.

Which brings us to the next step toward arriving at a fair and equitable solution to the current Health Care Crisis facing America.

It is imperative that we take an honest look at how we *ought* to be paying our medical bills in contrast to how we are paying them now. Only then, will we be in a position to focus our attention on, and target our expenditures at, physician-patient relationships that exclude government and business activities that needlessly inflate medical care costs.

As we have said. At the core of this solution is the return to a horizontally integrated health care system, where solo medical practices and physician organizations do the business of medicine in a fair and unconstrained, competitive market environment that is free of both government and politically powerful corporate influences.

In a nutshell, physicians and patients must be free to make all decisions regarding medical care; and, payments for all medical services must be under the control of patients, alone, without government or superfluous business meddling.

This kind of Health Care system would essentially constitute the "Gold Medal" model of Health Care. A system that could be up and running in less than a year following quick and responsible congressional and presidential action. The pessimistic old adage that "it will take an act of Congress" could be replaced by "*all it takes* is an act of Congress."

FIGURE 10 on the next page is a summary of the 2010 FEDERAL BUDGET EXPENDITURES OF UNITED STATES OF AMERICA.

FIGURE 10

**2010 FEDERAL BUDGET EXPENDITURES
OF THE UNITED STATES OF AMERICA**
($3,721 billion)

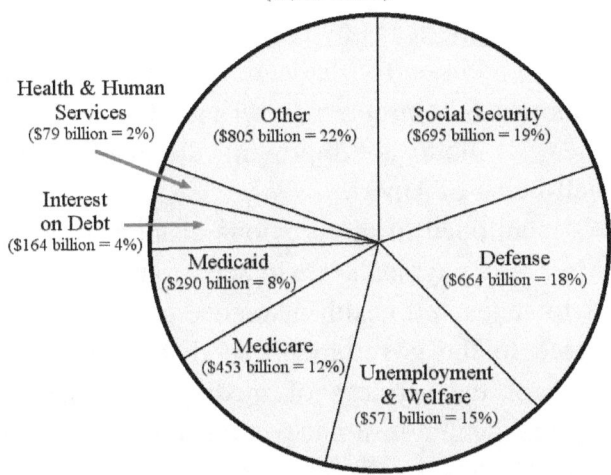

NOTE: Total revenues collected by the federal government amounted to
$2,165 billion, leaving a deficit of approximately $1,556 billion.

As shown in the graph, the combined cost of Medicare (federal assistance to individuals) and Medicaid (federal assistance to states) amounted to $743 billion, or approximately 20% of the total expenditures of the federal government in that year. These sums constitute the bulk of expenditures budgeted by the United States Department of Health and Human Services (HHS), which until 1979 was known as the Department of Health, Education, and Welfare (HEW).

The HHS serves as the Cabinet level department of the federal government that administers and monitors more than 300 programs and services in addition to Medicare and Medicaid. These programs include health and social science research, disease prevention and immunization services, health information technology databases like the CDC, and substance abuse treatment and prevention programs, to list a mere several. HHS has the responsibility to protect the health of all Americans by providing essential human services. In addition to Medicare and Medicaid, HHS spent another $78 billion monitoring all of its service branches. Its motto is "Improving the health, safety, and well-being of America."

As mentioned in the previous chapter, Medicare and Medicaid payments are made from federal accounts to states and health insurance companies subcontracted to the government, so that these entities can pay for the services of medical providers. Of course, the health insurance companies take "their cut" for assisting in the spending of your Medicare (payroll tax deductions that started coming out of your paycheck the first day you started working as a teenager) and Medicaid withholdings. And, as previously mentioned, both Federal (HHS) and State (Medicaid programs) government officials earn *their* salaries from related accounts for their role in processing -- and passing judgments upon -- the same claim forms your physician submits to them and health insurance companies in duplicate, triplicate, and quadruplicate.

What exactly are the total "medical operating costs" charged to us by health insurance companies, and related state and federal departments, in charge of paying those bills?

First, let us consider the "medical operating costs" drawn from "total premiums received" by vertically integrated health insurance companies shown in FIGURE 6 on page 151.

Let us assume that the total "percent operating costs" -- 17% -- shown in that chart for "the top seven health insurance conglomerates" was about the same for all health insurance companies. This is not an unreasonable assumption. Since, the top seven health insurance companies own substantial -- if not majority -- stock interests in almost all the other smaller health insurance companies; and, therefore, have a say in the accounting procedures and practices employed by those smaller companies. In any case, most businesses providing the same or similar pro-ducts and services tend to have the same overhead, expenses, and profit margins.

Secondly, consider again FIGURE 8 on page 155.

According to that graph, excluding about $250 billion in "out of pocket" expenditures made by individuals, there was a total of nearly $1.5 trillion in payments for medical claims made by private health insurance companies and Medicare and Medicaid programs for personal medical care services rendered by the medical community. One can assume that that figure -- taken from the most recent CDC study available -- has inflated since 2008. Had health care industry expenditures increased at a modest rate of 6% since then, we could calculate "the total personal health care expenditure by source of funds for 2010" (excluding those "out of pocket" expenditures made to physicians by individuals) to amount to $1.685 trillion ($1.5 x 1.06 x 1.06). If that were the case, then the sum of all "total premiums received" by the nation's health insurance companies and payroll deductions received from individual American taxpayers by the HHS managed Medicare/Medicaid programs to have been $2.03 trillion. Since, $2.03 trillion less 17% spent on "medical operating costs" ($345 billion) equals $1.685 trillion.

Now imagine that in that 2010, the HHS *had been* (a) put in charge of the bill paying services currently provided by health insurance conglomerates (that charged 17% in administrative costs) and their federal and state doppelgängers. Imagine also that (b) the premiums that we, and our employers, paid to those health insurance companies and Medicare/Medicaid programs were placed in *individual health care savings accounts* set up by the HHS, instead of us paying those premiums to health insurance companies and our existing Medicare/Medicaid Programs. And finally, and just as importantly, that (c) we -- as individual citizens -- *had had exclusive control over how we spent that money for medical services rendered without interference by the HHS*. In other words, that we and our physicians made all decisions regarding our personal medical care, and that *neither government officials nor health insurance company employees* -- who would no longer be collecting our premiums -- *had anything to say about how much we paid our doctors out of those personal health care savings accounts*.

We would, in effect, have increased the 2010 budget of the HHS -- to make all medical care payments from our *Individual Health Care Savings*

(IHCS) accounts from the $743 billion -- previously made available to make Medicare/Medicaid payments -- to $2.03 trillion to make all our medical care payments.

The cost of administering medical claims submitted directly to HHS by physicians for payment by our IHCS accounts could be reasonably estimated to have been no more than 2% of that budget (0.02 x $2.03 trillion = $41 billion) *in lieu* of the 17% (0.17 x $2.03 trillion = $345 billion) that would have otherwise have been "absorbed" by health insurance conglomerates and their federal doppelgängers in that year. A value of 2% in HHS administrative costs is not unreasonable when we consider that (1) the total administrative costs of the Social Security Administration -- which managed a budget of $695 billion in 2010 was a mere 0.9% of that department's total expenditures, and (2) that HHS administrators would no longer be wasting *their* time and *our* money making "judgments" regarding the medical care bills remitted by our physicians. Unlike the activities of present-day Medicare/Medicaid government officials, the "bill paying" responsibilities of HHS personnel -- under the new system -- would be confined to processing payments without interfering in the decisions already made and approved by doctors and their patients. One can easily imagine a high-speed computerized "bill paying service" coordinated by the HHS that could drastically reduce even more amounts once "soaked up" by health insurance companies. After accounting for 2% in administrative costs for HHS management of our IHCS account payments in 2010, the remaining amount available for remittance to physicians would have been about $1.989 trillion (0.98 x $2.03 trillion). Given the fact that a total of only $1.685 trillion in payments in medical claims would have been required to cover all of our medical bills, there would have remained a surplus of $304 billion in the HHS-IHCS General Fund.

That sum would be more than enough for the HHS to (a) monitor, "red flag," and prosecute physicians and patients attempting to defraud the system: much like the Internal Revenue Service does with its administrative budget of less than 0.5% of revenues collected from taxpayers. In addition, surplus sums could (b) be invested in United States Treasury Bonds (as is currently done with surplus Social Security funds), or in sound medical research and development programs, and interest earned then set aside to monetarily reward individuals who consistently act in defense of their own good health. This practice would surely (c) lead to further reductions in national health care expenditures by giving a fiscal incentive to a motivated citizenry who worked harder at preventing the onset of subacute and chronic medical conditions. This would be the most significant benefit of the new horizontally integrated American Health Care system, a welcome "side effect" that would result in further reductions in the exorbitant medical care expenditures that currently plague our Health Care system.

The creation of a fair and free market, ubiquitously accessible health care system in which every citizen had total control of their HHS-IHCS account, monies deposited and used for their private medical use, instead of being paid to the health insurance industry for the "bill paying services" they presently render, would have the following medical and monetary benefits.

Patients would (1) seek out physicians who provided the best, most compassionate, and least expensive medical care, (2) be proactive in defense of their own good health by following their doctors advice on a regular basis in an effort to reduce the incidence of subacute disease and the likelihood of developing costly chronic disease, and (3) reap the financial benefits awarded them for their healthy lifestyles.

From the start of this presentation, we have suggested -- and in subsequent pages have sought to emphasize -- that the achievement of excellent and affordable Health Care for the citizens of America will depend upon our willingness to reward the positive behaviors of the individuals whom we refer to as the *triad for Health Care*: (1) clinically astute and compassionate physicians, (2) scientists and engineers who produce new and innovative medical technology, and (3) patients motivated and proactive in defense of their own good health.

As shown below, the creation of the horizontally integrated, fair and free market Health Care system described above would inevitably provide us with the highest quality of medical service and state-of-the-art delivery of medical diagnosis and treatment made possible by modern technology. While at the same time, such a system -- by design in a fair and free market economy -- would reign in the out-of-control costs of today's Health Care system and significantly reduce those costs.

Adam Smith could, once again, rest in peace.

So, allow us to clearly define the operative terms used in the brief economic analysis that follows.

In that analysis, we use the term *technology* to mean the "state-of-the-art technology for diagnosis and treatment with diagnostic imaging/laboratory tests, and pharmaceutical/surgical treatments dictated by evidence-based medical research." We use the term *service* to mean the "caring, responsiveness, and altruism for the patient manifested by physicians adhering the complete intellectual application of the *Hippocratic Oath.*" We use the phrase *clinical astuteness* to mean the "diagnosis and treatment ability of physicians with excellent basic clinical skills for performing physical examinations at the bedside and obtaining patient history while minimizing the need and use of unnecessary technology." We use the phrase *health care* to mean "the maintenance of a person's well-being." We use the phrase *medical care* to mean the "health care rendered by physicians working in a fair and free market medical service industry." And, we use the term *cost* to mean "the money we spend as a nation on health care."

Using these terms, it is clear that health care can be seen as having three primary components as the well-being of patients is dependent upon all three in addition to the cost:

1. **Clinical Astuteness**
2. **Technology**
3. **Service**

As mentioned in the *Introduction*, when monetarily quantifying diagnosis and treatment, approximately 10 to 25 cents of each dollar is physician related, while 75 to 90 cents is strictly technology-driven.

Let us imagine for a moment that <u>only</u> technology were utilized in the delivery of medical care (the health care rendered by physicians), and that the involvement of physicians (their clinical astuteness and service) were eliminated. Then, medical care (the health care rendered by physicians) would be tantamount to technology. Since cost -- today -- is almost completely driven by technology (75-90 cents on the dollar), cost would be proportionate (~) to medical care.

Medical Care = Technology
Cost ~ Technology
Cost ~ Medical Care

This hypothetical health care model (health care without physicians) is <u>not</u> altogether "hypothetical." Since, the rising costs of Health Care in America are intimately linked to the rising costs of modern day medical technology. There is a linear relationship between rising Health Care costs and the costs incurred by our increasing use of that technology. As our use of technology increases, the cost of our medical care increases.

However, health care in America *should not be* synonymous with technology! It should, instead, be synonymous with medical care: the maintenance of well-being that is planned, initiated, and directed by a well-trained, competent, moral, and caring physician. In that type of health care system, a system that does not exist in today's America, the use of technology as the component that contributes most to ever-increasing health care costs would be significantly diminished as clinical astuteness and service take its place. In this type of health care system, the relationship of the three primary health care components listed above, as they pertain to medical care, is clearly summative and can be expressed as follows:

Medical Care = Clinical Astuteness + Technology + Service

In a competitive, horizontally integrated, fair and free market health care industry -- in which physicians' clinical astuteness and service must manifest at low cost in order to attract willing patients who value the money they have deposited in their HHS-IHCS accounts -- any reduction in the use of costly technology must reduce the overall cost of medical care! When well-trained, competent, moral, and caring physicians are put to work in such a system, the dollar amount of delivering health care must decrease.

The cost of health care is highly variable and dependent on service, clinical astuteness, and technology. And, the only way to reduce present health care costs in the long-term is to make the delivery of medical care highly efficient. Again, this can only be accomplished when medical care is based on the highest quality of training and the intellectual honesty of doctors, their respectable ethics, and their high degree of morality and altruism: as originally conceived by Hippocrates.

Physicians who are highly trained in clinical diagnosis and treatment, and who view technology, based on their clinical astuteness, as an aide to their clinical skill and not as an absolute, are less reliant on that same technology to diagnose and treat patients. This would inevitably result in better care at less cost. It is most critical and necessary for physicians to recognize the limitations of our present technology and to return to the basic skills utilized by the founding father of medicine, Hippocrates, in their physical diagnoses and ascertaining of their patients medical history. Alternatively stated: "When in doubt, look at the patient." The clinical astuteness of the physician is an integral part of the service aspect of delivering high quality medical care.

To restate the obvious: (1) Since medical care costs are significantly affected by technology, *cost decreases with better service and more significantly with enhanced clinical astuteness*. And (2), since enhanced clinical astuteness of well-trained and competitive physicians (who lack the kind of cognitive dissonance experienced by physicians working in our vertically integrated health care system) can reduce the frequency at which unnecessary technology is utilized, the *costs of medical care will decrease*.

In other words, as medical care improves costs decrease. The two become inversely proportional!

Costs ~ 1/Medical Care

By restoring choice of physician to the patient, demands on the practicing physician would be equally simplified. That is, in a fair and free, horizontally integrated health care system, doctors would be both more compelled and free to actually implement and practice the intellectual, moral, and ethical standards set forth twenty-four centuries ago in the *Hippocratic Oath*.

More important than the monetary gains to be reaped by our economy, from the savings we accrue with the diminishing costs of medical care, would be the enhanced joy our citizenry would experience by having a more healthful quality of life, by knowing the sheer satisfaction and excitement that comes with daily living through renewed mental and physical well-being.   That would be the most treasured achievement of the system of Health Care proposed below and worth more than all the money in the Treasury.

****

A SOLUTION TO THE
HEALTH CARE CRISIS FACING AMERICA

Eligible Citizens

All individuals in the United States (i.e., including birth citizens, naturalized citizens, and foreign visitors reimbursed by the HHS-IHCS General Fund) will be eligible to approve payments from HHS-IHCS accounts to pay for those medical services that they and their physicians deem practical and necessary.

Participating Physicians

All physicians (i.e., MD, DO, etc.) will be licensed in the United States: (A) National Medical Licensed (issued by US Government), (B) Individual State Registration issued by states, (C) National DEA issued by US Government.

All physicians will be permitted to see any patient in the United States in any state for which the physician has Individual State Registration. All physicians of the United States will have complete *Educational and Professional Vita* on a *National Medical Internet* documenting medical school attendance location and training, graduation year, location and durations of internship and residency, location and duration of fellowship training, location and durations of research work, list of scientifically and medically relevant publications, dates and outcomes of malpractice hearings and disciplinary actions.

Payers and Benefits

All individuals in the United States of America will have IHCS accounts from which medical payments are disbursed by the HHS; including those citizens considered "impoverished" under current tax laws, until such time as the economy and new tax laws make it possible for them to share the tax burden carried by their fellow citizens. This obligatory financial assistance would be consistent with the goals of any effectively functioning preventative health care system in which medical care is viewed as a "necessity" as opposed to a "right" or "privilege." Such practice would reduce the overall costs of health care in America by maintaining the general health of the populace at large.

Payments for all medical services -- dutifully agreed upon by patients and their physicians -- will be promptly remitted without dispute by the HHS from the HHS-IHCS General Fund and entered as a debit from the charging citizen's IHCS account. Citizens will be notified annually of the status of their deposits, debits, and account balances, as well as interest accrued (if any) to their account.

The HHS will have the authority to subcontract independent medical record-keeping companies assigned to protect the confidentiality of patients (similar to those companies currently protecting individuals against the threat of identity theft), and "spot audit" those otherwise confidential medical records of doctors and their patients to "red flag" and identify, investigate and criminally prosecute, cases of fraud with respect to patient care and outcomes. Patients and doctors will be notified that such records are being audited.

Any citizen wishing to "opt out" of the new system of universal health care may do so at their peril and will be held solely and legally liable for the costs of any medical services rendered (i.e., in both regular care and emergency situations). Citizens "opting out" may be required by physicians and physicians' groups to post a bond in amounts determined by those providers to insure that full payments made to them for medical services rendered are made without delay. This provision will preclude doctors from having to raise fees on those with IHCS accounts in order to cover the cost of litigation to collect monies owed them from those without IHCS accounts.

Medical Fees

While physicians and physicians' hospitals -- as well as other medical professionals, pharmacies and pharmaceutic-al firms -- may choose to charge fees they think reasonable and competitive, standardized fees will be suggested and published nationally by respected medical and other scientific organizations who may weigh them according to location in the United States, its territories and commonwealths.

Specific Individual Health Care Savings Accounts and the HHS-IHCS General Fund

A. Three thousand dollars ($3,000) will be placed into every new citizen's HHS-IHCS account by the US Treasury at birth.

B. Additional sums will added by individuals and their employers (as is now done under current Medicare/ Private insurance programs) into HHS-IHCS accounts in amounts set by Congress (as is now done under current Social Security and Medicare programs).

C. There will be option for individuals to place additional amounts into their personal account that will accrue additional interest on investments made by the HHS-IHCS General Fund.

D. Interest earned by investments of the HHS-IHCS General Fund will be placed in reserve for proper disbursement to investing individuals nearing or at retirement age as stipulated by law.

F. Retirement age to be consistent with current Social Security/Medicare programs and reevaluated in consideration of the *United States Census*.

G. Not less that 10% and not more than 50% of the remaining balance of any IHCS account may be withdrawn for any use at the discretion of individuals satisfying legal retirement requirements. Congress will stipulate such percentages in consideration of interest earned by investment of surpluses placed in the HHS-IHCS General Fund.

H. Fifty percent (50%) of the remaining balance of any HHS-IHCS account will be inherited (non-taxed) by beneficiaries designated by a deceased person having reached the legal retirement age. Fifty percent (50%) will be returned to the HHS-IHCS General Fund.

J. Two thousand dollars ($2,000) will be paid by naturalized citizens to their IHCS account along with matching funds in the amount of $1,000 paid by the Treasury upon naturalization. The legal retirement age of any naturalized citizen will be derived according to a formula stipulated by law as a function of the number of years the new citizen paid federal taxes.

Conflict Resolution

Conflict Mediation Boards consisting of relevant scientists, physicians, lawyers will resolve all patient-physician conflicts (i.e., medical, financial, malpractice, discipline). Participants sitting on such panels will be knowledgeable of the latest medical research and standards of care delivery, and have a general knowledge of all medical disciplines, including the legal, moral, and ethical dilemmas that accompany each area of care. They will be free of all financial and legal conflicts of interest with the parties named in malpractice claims filed before them. The Board will evaluate and render judgments within 3 months of the submission of a complaint. Appeals to a second and fresh group of mediators will be adjudicated within 6 months. All monetary and disciplinary judgments will be subject to binding arbitration.

****

In spite of the political times and the seemingly overwhelming obstacles we face as a Nation, Health Care *as it could be* provided in America holds enormous promise and potential for the future. But, it will be necessary to give fair and honest consideration to where we are today and where we wish to be tomorrow.

We have suggested a course of action that we believe will serve our Nation's best interests. A solution worthy of the American people, whose dedication to the principles of liberty, equality, and harmony, remains the envy of the civilized world. And in light of these ideals, we have been asking ourselves from the start of our deliberation of these issues a question all of us should ponder.

What would the Founding Fathers do?

Chapter 8
What Would The Founding Fathers Do?

****

Abstract

The health care crisis facing America has spawned a political debate that seems to be getting us nowhere. But our Founding Fathers, who faced more perilous challenges, knew exactly where they wanted to go. For decades prior to the American Revolution, they had evaluated the new thinking that arose from the *Renaissance* and the *Enlightenment* and concluded that it was time to abandon the dictatorial monarchies of the Old World and ride the wave of human progress toward a newer and freer way of life. If we are to remain worthy of their efforts and work together to solve the scores of problems that face us and the future of all peaceful peoples around the globe, we must abandon old attitudes and embrace the promise of new ideas. Given our own faltering financial system, and the outdated mindset of hapless politicians who cling to old arguments that make it impossible for them to "think outside the box," it seems to many that we as a Nation have become less and less likely to find solutions to those problems. Chief among our own Nation's problems is the calamity of rising medical care costs. Costs that cripple our economy and siphon wealth from the tasks we must perform to keep our Nation strong. The Founding Fathers would have found this situation intolerable and would have made it their first priority to insure that the health of every American was viewed, neither as a "right" nor as a "privilege, but as "necessary" to the survival of our democracy. They would have considered this single task to be as important to the health of the body politic as the preservation of the vast material resources, which this great land provides, and the liberty we so honorably hold dear. Shuffling off our present wasteful system of Health Care and replacing it with a fair and free market system is a national goal that must be achieved without delay, in order to *"secure the blessings of liberty to ourselves and our posterity!"*

****

It is worth noting that we, the authors, come from what today would be described as opposite poles of the political spectrum. Collen is a registered Republican and Handwerker is a registered Democrat. Yet, we both con-sider our tenuous party affiliations as secondary to the fact that we are both Americans. As did the Founding Fathers, we both believe that the strength of our relatively young and free society rests on the vibrancy of a fair and freely competitive capitalist economy. And, we think that the implicit constitutional role of our Federal Government -- in an effort to *"establish justice, insure domestic tranquility, provide for the common defense, and promote the general welfare"* -- is to protect fair and free market competition for all goods and services. Contrary to the conduct recently exhibited by contemporary government officials -- who spend more time "consulting" with Wall Street economists and wealthy corporate campaign contributors than they do listening to their constituencies -- we hold fast to the notions that it is not the role of government to favor those few individuals and business organizations who provide those goods and services at the expense of those who consume them. It is the government's job to *protect competition and not competitors*.

The *Declaration of Independence* inspired a nation of "freely trading" hardworking farmers, merchants, artisans, and pioneers to take arms against the royal families that enslaved the population of Europe. They seized the opportunity to create a fairer system of government. A government under which the solution to a nation's problems rested not with those few who laid claim to power by virtue of inherited wealth but with those for whom the ideals of individual liberty, freedom of action, diligence and creative innovation were paramount. Our Founding Fathers realized that for a people given the liberty to think and do as they please -- as long as the rights of their fellow Americans were not infringed -- that virtually nothing was impossible. Within a century, the inhabitants of the original thirteen colonies and their descendants, under a new and revolutionary form of democratic government expanded their influence over a continent. As millions flocked to America's shores in the centuries to come -- seeking protection under the *Constitution of The United States* -- that model of government has spread across the globe to enrich the lives of billions. But at the start of the 21st Century, following a century that will go down in history as among the most bloody and violent of periods yet to disgrace the likes of men, America still has considerable work to do.

Just as our Founding Fathers rebelled against tyranny in the body of a monarch who believed himself descended from a god, we are repulsed by super-wealthy plutocrats who deem themselves entitled to subvert our *Constitution* -- through the actions of the politicians who kowtow to them -- for the purpose of commandeering more than their fair share of America's material and economic bounty. Most Americans have known for generations that politicians and wealthy monopolists "are in bed together" and "walking hand-in-hand-to the bank" to deposit cash they have unethically and unscrupulously squeezed out of our economy. The astonishing difficulties we are having, today, stem from the fact that they are behaving -- publicly! -- like two drooling dogs in heat that refuse to be separated by the coldest bucket of showering ice water.

It is not just time for a change. It is imperative that we do change!

In order to appreciate how the fair and equitable solution to the Health Care crisis proposed in the last chapter can be quickly and successfully implemented -- despite the obstructing political forces that will certainly gather to thwart it -- it would be of value to briefly summarize the tumultuous history of the last bloody century. We do this in order to ascertain the forces that have fostered the current inability of our politicians to solve the Health Care Crisis, thus far, as well as other problems faced by our nation in this challenging new century.

When we view the long panorama of history, we find much of humanity's discontent to have arisen from conflicts between one group of humans and another: particularly in the form of struggles between chieftains and tribesman, lords and serfs, kings and subjects, haves-and-have-nots. For millennia prior to the late 18th Century, until the American Revolution, societies all over the world remained stuck in their ways, their cultures static and one dimensional in their peoples' social, political, and economic frames of mind. There were rulers and their "subjects;" or rather rulers and their "objects" with which those rulers could do pretty much as they pleased. Until the American Revolution, the people of Europe and the rest of the world labored in societies enmeshed in old habits of autocratic oppression, societies where the masses accepted their lot as the objects of oppressive aristocratic regimes.

But with the unabridged waters of the Atlantic to the East, and an expanse of open land more than twice the size of the European continent spreading attractively before them to the West, the American people seized the opportunity to cast off the old and meet the challenges of an unknown and exciting new future. It was the people of the American colonies, who came to choose, uncompromisingly, the liberating ideas of the *Renaissance* and *Enlightenment*. It was the people of the American colonies who took up arms against the aristocratic numskulls who ruled the British Isles and European and Eurasian continents at the time. Within decades, the rest of Europe would follow our example and revolt against the tyrannical status quo. And, having put the monarchs and nobles of Europe in their place, the colonists created a government *"of the people, by the people, and for the people."* Americans chose to embrace and nurture the revolutionary new idea of genuine cultural evolution and seized the opportunity to create true and lasting political and economic change through freedom of thought, freedom of action, and freedom of trade. It is thoroughly unsurprising that the United States of America, after less than two centuries following the drafting of our *Declaration of Independence*, became the most innovative, industrious, and wealthiest nation on the face of the Earth.

With experimentation in the discipline of fair and free market trade, the economic system we call *capitalism* became entrenched around the globe as the most successful model and strategy for political, economic, and cultural progress. Under that system, individual entrepreneurs -- rather than ruling aristocracies or state bureaucracies -- who could provide needed products and services for profit were put in control of a nation's industrial production and trade policies; while the peoples of other nations still longed to free themselves of the remaining aristocracies and super-wealthy autocracies of the world: oligarchies for whom a fair and free market economy -- an economy that rewards innovation and fair competition -- always represent a threat. To this day, the experiment conceived by our Founding Fathers is still called just that: *The American Experiment*. Since it is an experiment that -- if not fervently endorsed and painstakingly nurtured -- could easily go awry.

The great successes of the capitalist innovators of the 18th and 19th Centuries grew the American economy; but, at times, also threatened to hinder its fair and free expansion.

As discussed in *Chapter 5*, the unbridled greed of wealthy monopolists of the 19th and 20th Centuries, a newly spawned *nouveau riche*, has replaced the old landed gentry that once ruled Europe. Their efforts to protect their wealth, by impeding the attempts made by others struggling to position themselves in a fair and free marketplace, left many an innovator groveling under the heels of magnates who came to wield extraordinary political power. A thriving and growing, manufacturing and merchant middle class is nothing less than a threat to any plutocratic elite. Such an elite must take full possession and control of the wealth of creative producers -- by hook or crook -- in order to retain their wealth and power. President Theodore Roosevelt's efforts to rid the United States of the existing monopolies of his time, by enforcing the *Sherman Act*, is just one example of past democratic efforts directed at preserving a fair and competitive free market.

Then came the rival economic theory called communism. From 1922 until 1991, *communism* in the Soviet Union represented a rather sorry effort to shuffle off the oppression of the super-wealthy elite: as the ideals of communist leaders were drastically flawed.

Under a communist system, so taught Karl Marx the system's original advocate, the possessors of a society's greatest wealth must be brought down. It was necessary under such a system for all private property to be deemed publicly owned, and for each person to work and be paid according to their needs and abilities. The efforts of communists to bring "fairness" to the peoples of the world "naturally" and justifiably backfired: for a few very simple reasons.

To achieve their ideals, a method of *central planning by government elite* -- an elite that would insure the proper obtaining and distribution of a nation's resources -- would be needed to "control trade" and the "unfair and unbalanced" accumulation of wealth. Of course, the phrase "control trade" implies that trade is no longer free. It is controlled. And, where there are "legal limits" to freedom of action -- as opposed to common sense regula-tions that protect competition -- there may be no freedom at all. In addition, there is nothing morally or ethically wrong with the "accumu-lation of wealth." What is morally and ethically wrong is the using of that wealth to control govern-ment officials who make our laws and administer our democratic institutions.

Socialism, Marx augured, was to serve as the transitional phase between the overthrow of capital-ism (fair and free trade of private property) and the realization of the communistic ideal (elite government control over the distribution of communal property). Socialism comprises a political and economic theory of social organization that promotes a means of pro-duction, distribution, and trade that must be owned and regulated by the community as a whole. Of course at the time that Karl Marx published his works with Friedrich Engels in 1848, the violently oppressed peoples of Russia had little choice but to rebel against the inequalities imposed upon them by the stubborn and entrenched aristocracy of their country. In 1917 -- 34 years after the death of Marx in 1883 -- they chose to embrace socialism as a transition to commu-nism and what they believed would be the kind of freedom experienced by the democratically governed peoples of the Western economies.

With the success of the Russian Communist Revolution in 1917, the American model of capitalism had a rival and powerful new adversary. The 20th Century began with the pitting of capitalist world leaders in Europe and America against socialist leaders in the Soviet Union. The people of the world were asked to choose between two diametrically opposing economic ideologies whose single indistinguishable goal was -- ostensibly -- to advance the well-being of humankind.

Communism, which to many "seemed like a good idea at the time" -- and served the worthy purpose of ridding an oppressed society of its cruel and domineering "royal aristocracy" -- instead gave the Russian people a new and repressive "bureaucratic autocracy."

Perhaps, the successes of capitalism over communism arise from circumstances that make capitalism a decidedly more "natural" human endeavor. It seems that free trade may be more conducive to our survival as a set of adaptive human activities. As it is an economic system manifested by our "natural" desire to be social beings. Beings who wish to act freely yet find "sharing and sharing alike" beneficial to our own safety and peace of mind.

Of course, advocates of a communist/socialist system would claim the same human prerogative to "share and share alike" as basic to their social system. But, the practical outcomes of the two contrasting economic systems -- communism versus capitalism -- have been shown by historical events to be demonstrably different.

In a communist/socialist system it is the function of government to oversee the distribution of natural and monetary resources so that the allocation of those resources is achieved in an "egalitarian" way. This must be done, under such a system, to preclude the "unfair and unbalanced" accumulation of wealth. As a means to that end, the original guardians of the Russian Revolution created an elite bureaucracy of administrators to discharge the duty of disseminating their nation's wealth. To achieve this, the socialist elite deemed it necessary to restrict fair and free trade among the masses by placing sole responsibility for the distribution of goods in the hands of a few. Corrupt administrators who came to care more for their own fortunes and political status than for the misfortunes of their citizenry. In this respect, they resembled more the autocrats whom their revolution sought to destroy than the citizens whom their revolution sought to liberate. To those government administrators, the phrase "share and share alike," came to mean the "equalization of compensation" for all citizens of their country; so that, no individual could claim more wealth than any other individual. More often than not, this strategy also required that administrators be empowered to dictate the kinds of work people needed to do "for the betterment of the State," instead of freeing the populace to use their own initiative regarding the production and distribution of goods and services. This practice, in addition to the practice of equalizing compensation, drained the Russian workforce of its creative inspiration and capacity for innovation. Soviet citizens began to ask them self: "What is there to gain by working harder, or more imaginatively, to better a system that does not recognize the value of extra effort or novel ideas?"

By 1989, the people of Russia and its repressed satellite neighbors, as did the world's free peoples who already saw the writing on the wall, came to recognize these flaws of the communist/socialist system. The Russian people, once again, embraced the benefits of capitalism over those of a "centralized economy."

The Berlin Wall was reduced to rubble.

Under the economic system advocated by our Founding Fathers, however, it is the function of government to encourage its citizens to exercise their creative inspiration and capacity for innovation by protecting a fair and free market economy against any controlling elite descended from royalty or *nouveau riche*. Instead of land and material being held in the hands of a few, it became possible for every citizen to own property that they could trade freely for the betterment of all. Rather that being in charge of the distribution of wealth, it is the primary task of our elected officials to guarantee that all innovators and entrepreneurs play by the same rules, and that none has an unwarranted and unmerited advantage over others. Every one of us has the innate ability to sense when we are being cheated. And, as a democratic society we make laws to prevent dishonest tradesmen from swindling us; and, we do our best to punish those who make a habit of it. In a truly fair and free market capitalist system, it is the role of government to make laws that protect free trade and competition to the detriment of greedy individuals who lay claim to more than their deserved portion of a nation's monetary wealth and precious natural resources.

The role of those elected officials who assure us of their desire to "serve the public good" is -- in this respect -- much like the role of the modern physician. Instead of swearing to the *Hippocratic Oath* and to live by its tenets, our politicians swear to *"uphold the Constitution,"* and live by its injunctions to *"... establish justice, insure domestic tranquility, provide for the common defense, and promote the general welfare."* Like the modern physician who cares for the health of our bodies, we expect our elected officials to nurture the health of the body politic. Like physicians, our government representatives and those whom they appoint must faithfully demonstrate to the electorate that they possess the qualities of sincerity, compassion, and the desire to protect their constituencies against the ills of society manifested in the forms of selfishness, greed, and corruption.

Yet despite the clear and certain demise of the communist system, we arrive at the birth of the 21st Century, in which American political personalities and their parties still live in the past. We see and hear it everyday in the news as media talking heads and politicians trapped in the gory mindset of the 20th century lambaste one another with accusations such as "Ooh! You're a socialist!" ... or ... "Ooh! You're a fascist!" These mindless and mean-spirited epithets become the mating calls of misguided buffoons echoing off the rotunda of the Capitol Dome from both sides of the aisle. A hallowed place, where otherwise intelligent and patriotic individuals would never forget that "We are all Americans!"

We are faced with the reality that the dimensions of global politics in the 21st Century are no longer one-dimensional -- *communist versus fascist* -- as they were in the last century. They are "multidimensional." And, the problems that our leaders and we face at the dawn of this new millennium require a multidimensional approach and the capacity to "think outside the box" of constraining old ideals.

As the old adage says: *"If you always do what you've done you will always get what you've always gotten."*

In short, there is no sure-fire management strategy that will permit a complex society to flawlessly distribute the natural wealth and monetary resources of a nation. There is no political system in which leaders are always great or even mostly good. Just as there is no entirely true scientific theory able to predict all possible outcomes. There are always, however, opportunities for disaster to rear its ugly head. As matters of public policy, there are no purely rational courses of action that can always protect us from calamity. The only logical approach is to judge our public and private institutions and way of life by how successful we are at undoing the mistakes we make. In the United States of America, under the rules set forth in the Constitution, we can do this quite frequently by ousting bad leaders whose explanations of "why things are the way they are" are flawed, and whose "ways of doing things" keep getting us into trouble. It is time to start correcting our mistakes by *"ousting bad leaders"* and undoing the mistakes we -- and they -- continue to make.

In order to recover from the disaster we call Health Care, we will require the courage to change and risk making a few mistakes in order to transform a system whose continued existence will drive our nation into bankruptcy.

We believe that the Founding Fathers would agree. It is an essential characteristic of the American spirit to be wary of "factions and cabals" and to boldly pioneer into the unknown in expectation of overcoming whatever challenges the future might have in store. Problems test our national mettle. And our attitude toward them tests our worth as a free and benevolent people.

Since the days of the American Revolution, all true Americans have bravely faced the icy winds of change and withstood its tumultuous fury. Our *Constitution* welcomes change in the form of new laws and amendments that can help us solve new problems and right the wrongs of old mistakes. Thomas Jefferson relied upon the true nature of the American character, to expand the United States in wealth and breadth, when he broadened the horizons of every American's dreams with the purchase of the Louisiana Territory from France.

America is a nation of pioneers. Anyone hopelessly afraid of change is un-American. Anyone who would abandon the pioneer spirit in the name of a ramshackle *status quo* is un-American. Anyone who fears a challenge is un-American.

Is this proposed solution to the Health Care Crisis facing America a pipe dream?

Some may so claim. But, then again, in 1776, so was the American Revolution to the wealthy aristocrats loyal to King George.

The solution we have proposed to the Health Care Crisis facing America is not politically conservative, nor is it politically progressive, nor politically anything. It's just plain old American common sense. We are confronted with a modern aristocracy no less venomous than the one that ruled Europe before the American Revolution, factions and cabals that cling tight to the *status quo* and a collection of seemingly intransigent ideals that prohibits us from, once again, taking our place as leaders of the world among the other great industrial democracies in the spirit that our *Declaration of Independence* helped to cultivate.

We all see it. We all know it. In the names of our Founding Fathers, what will *"We The People..."* do about it?

We, the authors, propose that we all get off our butts and change things. And, make no mistake. This *is* an American Revolution.

END

Information Resources

The former Vice-President of the United States of America, Al Gore, once lost political points for having quipped that he had "invented the Internet." He based this rather audacious claim on the fact that he did, indeed, author some of the critical legislation that made the Internet and World Wide Web possible. However, if Former Vice-President Gore had the right to claim credit for anything having to do with such an astounding scientific achievement, it might have been the simple fact that -- at the time of the invention of the Internet -- he was a proud American living in a free society where laws promoting freedom of expression, including the freedom to innovate, are cherished above all our unalienable Rights. The real credit for inventing the Internet, of course, goes to the thousands of mathematicians, scientists, and engineers who throughout the centuries exercised their own freedom of thought to achieve remarkable ends. As a result of their efforts, work that included the labors of many outstanding Americans, the citizens of our Nation, as well as in every democratized society around the globe, are now free to travel the information superhighway without hindrance from despotic oligarchs. For this reason, the authors found little need to scrupulously cite the source of every iota of information used in factually documenting and presenting this solution to the current Health Care Crisis facing America. In gathering the data required to support our conclusions, we -- like all inquisitive Americans -- availed ourselves of the vast library of printed and electronically stored information at our fingertips. Anyone with a computer and access to the WWW may do as we did and search the Web to verify the information presented in this work. We do recommend, however, that anyone choosing to do so corroborate the data they find with no less than two additional reliable Internet and literary sources made available to us through the courtesy of the *First Amendment* to *The United States Constitution* which insures our right to a free press.

About the Authors

Martin J. Collen is a "Republican" AMERICAN, born in Oakland, California, and raised in Los Angeles. He is an internationally recognized physician who, for more than 30 years, has practiced "the art and science of medicine" according to the tenets of the *Hippocratic Oath*. He is the author of more than 250 original research and review publications, including books, articles, and abstracts. He graduated with a BA in Mathematics from UCLA in 1966, and attended Chicago Medical School at Rosalind Franklin University of Medicine and Science, Chicago, Illinois, graduating with an MD degree in 1970. He completed a year of internship in medicine and a year of residency in General Surgery at UCI, and went on to complete an additional two years of residency in Internal Medicine and a two year Fellowship in Gastroenterology at UCLA until 1977. He was an Assistant Professor of Medicine at UCI, from 1977 to 1980, and Instructor of the Year for two successive years. He completed a research Fellowship in Gastroenterology from 1980 to 1985 at the National Institute of Health in Bethesda, Maryland, and was Associate Professor of Medicine and Director of Gastrointestinal Research at Georgetown University Medical Center in Washington, D.C., from 1985 to 1990. He moved back to California in 1990, where he was Professor of Medicine at Loma Linda University from 1990 to 1995 and Clinical Professor of Medicine from 1995 to 2005. He earned an Executive MBA in Health Care from UCI in 1999. Since 1995, he has been in private practice as a gastroenterologist in the Inland Empire. Dr. Collen lives with his wife, Roberta, and their youngest of four children in Riverside, California.

Mark J. Handwerker is a "Democratic" AMERI-CAN, born in Brooklyn, New York, and raised in three of the five boroughs of the Big Apple. He is a teacher and writer with more than a dozen publications, including books and articles in a number of scientific fields. He graduated with a BS from CCNY in Psychology/Biology and moved to California in 1972 were he attended UCI, graduating with a PhD in Biology in 1976. He began teaching for the Los Angeles Unified School District in 1982 until accepting a position with the Temecula Valley Unified School District in 1988, where he continues to teach young people the basic methodology and principles of science once esteemed and put into practice by the courageous Founders of this Nation. Dr. Handwerker lives with his wife, Judith, in Riverside, California.